Concrete Connections
Building Solid Relationships That Last

By
Charles Woods

Co-authored by Powerful Relationship Builders

2024

Use the QR code to access Charles Woods' online store!!!

Copyright © 2024 by Charles Woods

All rights reserved. This book or any portion thereof may not be reproduced or used in any manner whatsoever without the express written permission of the publisher except for the use of brief quotations in a book review or scholarly journal.

First Printing: 2024

ISBN: 979-8-9900725-4-1

Ordering Information:

Special discounts are available on quantity purchases by corporations, associations, educators, and others. For details, contact the publisher at the email listed below.

U.S. trade bookstores and wholesalers:
Please contact woodzworxgroup@gmail.com

DEDICATION

Concrete Connections is dedicated to the relationships that we have built over the years with the individuals and family members that take the time to love us and support our efforts. We look forward to maintaining our strong relationships and building an even stronger future. We know that we are not perfect and are only as strong as the bonds that we have with the important individuals in our lives. We are grateful for these concrete connections!!!

PREFACE

Dear Reader,

Nothing in life is accomplished in isolation. We are inspired by the relationships that we build and the growth that is achieved because of those strong relationships. Through our chapters, we will discuss the importance of relationships from our individual points of view and how these relationships have fostered a positive difference in our lives and the lives of others. We hope to support you on your journey through life and assist you in effectively building and maintaining concrete connections!!!

Brief Description of Book

Relationships are a part of everyone's life, whether they are good or bad. This book is focused on strong relationships and how those relationships make a positive difference. When we establish positive relationships, the opportunities are limitless.

Concrete Connections, Building Solid Relationships That Last, is packed full of knowledge from an assortment of strong relationship builders. The authors will draw you into their world and supply you with a unique perspective of strong relationships from their personal life experiences. They will shed light on the importance of the bonds that are built and how those relationships will forever make a positive difference.

This powerful compilation highlights fifteen positive relationship builders that have grown through the relationships that they have fostered as they propel themselves and others forward in life. Everyone needs some type of support and the concrete connections that are created will provide that support. We are always better together!!!

Table of Contents

- DEDICATION iv
- PREFACE v
- Brief Description of Book v
- LIST OF AUTHORS IN CHAPTER ORDER vii
- THREE TIMES CONNECTED 1
- CONCRETE CONNECTIONS ARE POWERFUL 11
- FOSTERING POSITIVE PROFESSIONAL RELATIONSHIPS 17
- LET THEM LOVE YOU 23
- STRENGTH OF YOUR PILLARS 31
- NO ONE IS SELF-MADE 39
- THE ROAD TO BECOMING A CONNECTED CATALYST 47
- MENTORING & BUILDING STRONG RELATIONSHIPS 53
- THE PSYCHOLOGY OF RELATIONSHIPS 61
- BROTHERHOOD AND PURPOSE 67
- CALAIS CONNECTIONS 75
- A SON'S SUCCESS DRIVEN BY CONNECTIONS 83
- CONTINUE TO BECOME 91
- TRUST AS THE ESSENTIAL COMPONENT OF A LASTING RELATIONSHIP 99
- FORGING A CONNECTION WITH 107
- ABOUT THE LEAD AUTHOR 117

LIST OF AUTHORS IN CHAPTER ORDER

1. Charles Woods
2. Chip Baker
3. Dr. Denetria Phlegm
4. Derrick Pearson
5. Desmond Jones
6. Emory Hunt
7. Jessica Perez
8. Kenneth Wilson
9. Kristen Davis
10. Marquise Sneed
11. Michael Calais
12. Monica Earl Semple
13. Terri Walters
14. Dr. Troy Wingerter
15. Victor Pisano

THREE TIMES CONNECTED
Charles Woods

"Nothing is accomplished alone; however, everything can be accomplished through your connections!!!"
~Charles Woods

"Sometimes we forget about the importance of our connections, just checking on someone can go a long way!!!"
~Charles Woods

The Beginning of a Strong Connection

It was 1989 and my first year in Junior High School, which was the seventh grade to be more exact. This would be a pivotal year for me and my choice of friends primarily because there was a huge shift in my community. It was vital for me to make choices that would make my life better. This was an enormous responsibility and at that time, I had no idea about the importance of these decisions. Before school officially started, I decided to join the seventh-grade football team, mainly because I did not have the opportunity to play football for the community youth league plus my two close friends were going to participate. These gentlemen would be an important part of my life as we established a strong unique bond. Calvin Bennett and I started our bond in kindergarten at Runyan Elementary School. We lived in the same neighborhood for about two years, so we were able to grow our connection. As time went by my family would move and I started the third grade at a different elementary school. Calvin and I would see each other sporadically for a few years, but it was nothing like being at the same school and living in the same neighborhood.

In my new neighborhood, Demetrius Scott lived a few blocks up the road, which gave us many opportunities to bond. We had many commonalities that strengthened our relationship but the one that stood out the most was avoiding trouble. His father owned the neighborhood night club, so during the daytime, when the building was closed, we would spend hours pretending to be R&B singers and Hip-Hop artists. With the music turned up and the microphone volume turned low anything was possible.

When school started, we met Fabion Johnson and our group of three quickly became four. There was something about him that set him apart from others which made him a good fit for our exclusive group of friends. Fabian never put on a show, and he was a genuinely kind person. He was the type of person that would add value to our circle, and I know he felt the same about us. This was the start of an amazing connection.

We made it through Junior High School and our bond was tighter than ever. We were ready to take on the ninth grade with eager energy as we tackled all obstacles, but that was also when we faced a huge blow to our unique group of four. Demetrius broke his leg while we were playing touch football and eventually moved during the first month of school. We did not have cell phones, so it was quite easy to lose connection once someone moved. In our world this was a tragic event that threw us for a loop, but we quickly realized it was out of our control. Junior year, Derick Hobbs joined our special bond. We all played football, and in addition to those great experiences, Derick and I shared several amazing memories on the track. I had the privilege of handing off the relay stick to Derick in the 4x100 meter relay and the 4x400 meter relay. Hands-down, Derick was one of the best running around that 400-meter track and a GREAT friend.

It was finally our Senior year, and a young freshman named Rock Cartwright joined our tight connection. He was a five-star athlete that could play any sport but more than his athletic ability, he was an amazing young man and a GREAT addition to our unique group. He ended up playing college football and then played for over ten years in the NFL. We are extremely grateful for the life experiences that we had because of Rock. That senior year, we also saw more of our classmate Andre Williams. He was always around, but he connected with us more that year. Andre was a hardworking, intelligent young man that was focused on working and graduating. These were outstanding young men doing outstanding things while earning a public education. These were my brothers, and we were all like-minded kids with aspirations of having a better life.

I took time to mention these gentlemen and their short descriptor during this particularly important time in my life because this was when I learned how important it is to surround yourself with good positive people and hold on to those strong connections. We were a lucky group of young men that took care of each other. We all had struggles, issues, and heart aches but we held each other accountable and supported each other when needed. There is no telling where I would be without these gentlemen, and I know they would say the same about me. Please do not misunderstand me, we were not perfect, but each of our situations could have been worse.

The experiences I gained from this group of self-driven gentlemen were instrumental in me recognizing that life is about the connections that you make. Those connections allow you to genuinely support each other through your everyday ebbs and flows. The statement, "It takes a village" is very true, and it is not just about raising children. It takes a village for any individual to progress in life. No one makes it on their own!

Everyone should have a supportive circle filled with individuals that look out for one another. Individuals that are not afraid to let you know when you are being unrealistic or not using your best judgement. Individuals that will cheer for you when you are doing well and are not envious of your success. These types of relationships are not built around the quantity of people you know. These types of relationships are always built around the quality of the connections you establish. Energy and trust are the top ingredients for building strong relationships and these types of relationships survive because of that positive energy and unwavering trust. I am blessed to continue to have these gentlemen in my life, in their own unique ways.

An Unexpected Connection

After graduating with a bachelor's degree from the University of Louisiana at Lafayette, I began looking for a job in the oil and gas industry. The job market was not working in my favor and the interview process was very strenuous. About three weeks into my job search I received a phone call from Coach Tyke Tolbert, who was the wide receivers' coach at the University of Louisiana Lafayette. Coach Tolbert informed me that Coach Gary Bartel, my previous position coach, expressed his interest in me coming back to the University and being a graduate assistant football coach. Coach Tolbert also informed me that the athletic department would pay for my tuition, room, and board in a graduate program of my choice. I had no intention of going back to school for a master's degree, so this was a total shock. I needed a little time to think about my next move. It took me about ten minutes.

I called Coach Tolbert back to inform him that I was going to return to Lafayette and accept the graduate assistant position. This was an opportunity that I could not pass up. I was granted the chance to get a master's degree and coach football at my alma mater. This opportunity would open several doors for me. Not only would I have an opportunity to obtain gainful employment in the oil and gas industry, but I would also have the prerogative to pursue coaching jobs if that was my choice. Thinking about this opportunity, I realized that I owed everything to the relationships I had with the coaches at the University and one of the most amazing parts to this story was this was not the original coaching staff that recruited me. Coach Bartel was my third defensive back coach and Coach Jerry Baldwin was my second head football coach. There were things about that coaching staff that I did not like, but as a student athlete, I made it my priority to connect with all coaches.

I did not take things personal and made sure that I put myself in a position to be successful. My goal was to get a college degree, not to be liked. I was nominated team captain my senior year, and I was mature enough to take care of my responsibilities. My coaches never had to worry about me disrespecting them or not meeting program expectations. Those are some of the reasons I was afforded this opportunity. These graduate assistant positions were minimal, so being grateful for this opportunity is an understatement. I will say it again, I owed this chance of a lifetime to the relationships that I built with the football coaching staff and University of Louisiana Lafayette community. You never know what opportunities may come from the connections you create.

Staying Connected

The reason that I am in education started when I was a junior in high school. That year our football team went through a huge coaching change. We got a new head football coach, and our entire defensive staff had an overhaul. I played cornerback, so yes, I was getting a new position coach. To my surprise, my coach ended up being one of the coaches from the previous coaching staff, Coach Greg Poole. He coached wide receivers when I was a freshman and sophomore, so I was incredibly stunned when I found out that he would be our new defensive back coach. I admired my previous defensive back coach, Coach Chris Massey, so I went into this coaching change with uncertainties. What did he know about coaching defense? The only thing I saw him coach was offense. I had no idea what direction our defensive was going, but I knew this had to work out.

To my surprise, Coach Poole poured into me and my teammates. He made sure he built solid relationships with each of his players. He did everything expected and more. He ended up being a GREAT defensive back coach and we ended up building an amazing player coach connection.

Fast forward to 2002, I had just graduated from college with my master's degree and Coach Poole was now Dr. Poole. Coach Poole was no longer coaching, he was the Principal at Caney Creek High School in Conroe ISD. Looking for a lead in the oil and gas industry, I reached out to him. He cut me off midway through our conversation to say, I would make a great coach and teacher. I explained to Coach Poole that I did not want to teach anyone's kids, coach anyone's kids, and I did not want to talk to parents about their kids.

Coach Poole looked past my comments and continued to express how he thought that education would be a great fit for me. Out of respect for Coach Poole, and the relationship that we had, I accepted an interview. On the day of the interview, we were in his office for a limited amount of time before we took a tour of the campus. I noticed about two minutes into the tour that we were walking towards the athletics hallway. He walked me into the coach's office, where we noticed that there was a defensive meeting in the next room. Coach Poole gently nudged me into the room and stated, "We will find your teaching field later."

Again, out of respect for Coach Poole and our relationship, I informed him that I would try this teaching and coaching experience for a year and see where I stood at the end of the school year. It took me two weeks and I was hooked. I loved serving kids. I loved being in an environment where I could support the dreams and goals of young men and women. This was a monumental time in my life. I had chosen a career path and was about to start a new chapter.

This opportunity was not afforded to me because of my credentials, my degrees, or the experience that I did not have. I received this opportunity because someone believed in me and trusted that I was a good fit for this role. These types of opportunities only come from having concrete connections.

"A degree will ensure that you can accept a job, but the relationship will be the reason you get the job."
~Charles Woods

These three short stories are examples of concrete connections that aided in propelling me positively forward in life. These are the types of relationships that can make a difference in the lives of any individual that makes a conscious decision to create them. <u>The Beginning Of A Strong Connection</u> was a period where I learned about the type of people and energy I should let in. When evaluating my situation, I realized that there was something bigger for me in this world and I was going to do my best to ignite those opportunities. This positive movement started with the close like-minded friends that I allowed in my life.

- We were **G**RATEFUL to have each other.
- We were **R**ESILIENT, when faced with obstacles.
- Our **E**NERGY remained positive with each other in all situations.
- We were **A**CCOUNTABLE for our actions.
- We had a huge amount of **T**RUST for each other.

We were GREAT for each other and in control of our futures. The five traits emphasized above were instrumental in our connection and aided me in <u>An Unexpected Connection</u>. These GREAT traits were the framework for me connecting and maintaining strong relationships even when there were frustrations or concerns. These traits helped me build bonds that later assisted me in giving myself a better life and put me in a position where I could assist others. <u>Staying Connected</u> touched on a time when I learned to trust an individual that was outside my circle. An individual with which I had very few interactions. We worked hard to create our connection and the connection we created has survived through the test of time. This connection led to many important accomplishments throughout my life and the impact continues.

It is not easy to choose who you allow in your space, but these are important decisions that must be made. These decisions could have a significant impact on your life and/or the lives of those closest to you. Your mental well-being and physical safety are essential, and no one should be able to put those at risk. Being in the space of like-minded individuals with positive energy are GREAT connections to make and maintain as you protect your space. Always choose quality not quantity!!!

When focusing on building these connections, I utilize the Principles Of GREATness with a focus on the 5 traits of GREAT, intentionally highlighting Energy and Trust.

Principles Of GREATness:
Think GREAT!!! Do GREAT!!! Be GREAT!!!

5 traits of GREAT
1. **G**ratitude
2. **R**esilience
3. **E**nergy
4. **A**ccountability
5. **T**rust

Energy
- Positive Mindset
- Control what you can control.
- It is not about you.
- Be aware of your delivery.

Trust
- Have others' best interest in mind.
- Straightforward communication
- Be reliable.

- Individuals should be acknowledged and celebrated.
- Take time to personally check on others.
- Have good intentions.

When interacting with others, I make sure I own my behavior. My energy output will be positive with the intention of infecting others with that same energy. Life is simple but made difficult by the people of this world. I continue to work hard to maintain the strong relationships that I have created. I also enjoy developing new concrete connections with like-minded individuals that want to build solid relationships that last. *The three relationships mentioned above were only the beginning, but they made me three times better.* I continue to hear how relationships are important, but somewhere between the discussions and the implementation there lies a disconnect. The message about the importance of relationships somehow gets lost. Individuals begin to stop feeling valued by their companies or organizations and good people make a change. Friends and families go through turmoil because of miscommunication or a break in trust. Developing solid relationships and maintaining them must be a priority. Once you start building these relationships, it becomes easier to develop and maintain others. Please take time and focus on relationships. We are charged with doing a better job with these Concrete Connections as they are the foundation to individual and team success as well as a life filled with happiness!!!

ABOUT THE AUTHOR:
See Lead Author's Bio in About the Lead Author section.

CONCRETE CONNECTIONS ARE POWERFUL
Chip Baker

Picture this, visualize with me an extension cord plug going into a wall power socket. When plugged into the source, power flows through on the other end. Power flows through because the extension cord is connected to the source.

The source that helps us reach our maximum potential are our relationships. Relationships bring powerful connections. When we are connected so many great things happen, and we are able to continue that flow of power through our connections.

Relationships are important. They foster a positive difference in our lives. Relationships foster a positive difference in the lives of everyone that we encounter. It is powerful! It is concrete! We become connected!

"Relationships are the bridge to our everlasting impact."
~Chip Baker

Relationships are very important. No significant success is achieved alone. The fact that we are here and alive shows that relationships are important. That is how we were created. It literally gave us life.

Relationships help build bonds that last forever. As a child I grew up in a single parent household. Both parents were great people and present in my life, but I was raised in the home with my mother. I was fortunate enough to grow up around some amazing families that showed me how families should operate. Most of them had both parents in the house. I was able to observe and experience eating at the dinner table as a family, going out to outings as a group, and doing things in the home as a family. We experienced amazing things in my home. My mom was my superhero and did everything she could. She was amazing. She was also smart enough to know that it was important to put me around people that I could build concrete connections with. Those connections have created life-long relationships that are still mutually beneficial because we met at a young age. We have been in each other's weddings, taken family vacations together, helped each other navigate through tough times, and are still connected to this day because of the connections we created when we were kids. I love these men as my brothers because they have been there for me in the times when things were great. Most importantly, they have been there for me when I have been at my lowest points in life. I am truly grateful for them.

I thought that I had some amazing friends growing up in my hometown; however, when I got out of my box and went to college, I encountered even more amazing connections that have become concrete over the years. They were people from all backgrounds, all races, and all socioeconomic statuses. All were great people that I learned so much from. It was neat to have conversations with them to understand what it was like where they grew up. It was also cool to go and visit their hometowns to see how they grew up and meet their families. This experience was one that was life-changing for me because I saw the love that these families had for one another. I was tremendously grateful that they welcomed me in as family.

In college I tore my ACL in my left knee. Those same people stepped up and took care of me. They made sure that I had food and made it to all my classes. This was huge because they did not have to do that. They were there for me when I was not capable of fully taking care of myself. I have tried to return that by showing love and supporting them in all their endeavors over the years. It has caused us to have connections that are concrete and strong.

"Quality relationships make a difference."
~Chip Baker

Relationships have helped foster a positive difference in my life. As I reflect, those relationships have helped me immensely in my personal and professional life. I have learned so much. What I learned from these connections has allowed me the privilege of sharing similar experiences with my loved ones. It has also allowed me to operate in a manner to exhibit the things that I have learned in my daily actions. Professionally, these relationships have allowed me to learn many things that have resulted in opportunities and promotions. Some of those people, in those relationships, have believed in me when I did not even believe in myself. Each position I have had has come from someone having a great relationship with me and trusting that I could do a great job at the tasks given to me. I am grateful for people who have believed in me.

"Concrete connections create big accomplishments."
~Chip Baker

The biggest accomplishments I have been blessed to achieve in life have come from someone teaching me how to do it. They guided me and fostered my learning so that I could stay on the right path. It blows me away thinking about all the great things I have learned over the years. I recall the experience I gained from an older Coach that I had the pleasure of having a desk beside for twelve years of my career. He would say to me "Come with me and do this so that you can see how to do it. When we have to do it again, I will let you do it and guide you through. You will have to be able to do this one day."

That experience was priceless! That is just one example of many that I have experienced that has catapulted me to high heights.

"Life moves at the speed of our relationships."
~Pastor Danny Green

Relationships have allowed me to foster a positive difference in the lives of others. I am currently in the twenty-fourth year of my career in education. I coached for twenty of those years. I have been teacher of the year a couple times. I have a YouTube channel and podcast where I interview people from all walks of life to share their stories for positive inspiration and motivation. I have interviewed some amazing influencers. I am a multiple time bestselling author.

All those accomplishments are neat, I am grateful for them. But there is nothing better than experiencing those things, taking the lessons I learned from them, and then using them to be a blessing to others. This fills me up and makes me completely happy.

"Opportunities bring opportunities."
~Chip Baker

I am in the give-back phase of my life. I am in a space where I am striving to do everything to give back to others to help them move more efficiently and effectively. It has allowed me the opportunity to provide opportunities. It is not good enough for me to write books. I must help others write books too. It is not good enough for me to travel and speak to groups, organizations, and teams. I must help others have opportunities to live in their purpose and share their stories when speaking. It is not good enough for me to have concrete connections. I must establish and build relationships so that others have concrete relationships too.

I feel that by doing this I will not just leave a legacy when I get to go visit the "Big Man". It will let me live a legacy by my day-to-day actions.

In closing, relationships are important. They help to foster a positive difference in our lives. Relationships are key because they allow us to connect and have continued growth.

There are a couple questions that I want to ask you.
- Are you connected to the source?
- Are you connected to concrete relationships?

Quality relationships are the source that brings powerful connections. Just like that electrical plug, that power spreads and illuminates our world for generations. God bless you on your journey to create and build concrete connections.

Go get it!!!

ABOUT THE AUTHOR:

Social Media:
IG @chipbakertsc
FB @chipbakertsc
Email chipbakertsc@gmail.com

Chip Baker is a fourth-generation educator. He has been a teacher/coach for over twenty-three years. He is a multiple-time best-selling Author, Youtuber/Podcaster, Motivational Speaker and Life Coach.

Chip Baker is the creator of the YouTube channel/podcast "Chip Baker - The Success Chronicles" where he interviews people from all walks of life and shares their stories for positive inspiration and motivation.

Live. Learn. Serve. Inspire. Go get it!

Chip Baker Books
Growing Through Your Go Through
Effective Conversation to Ignite Relationships
Suited For Success Vol. 2
The Formula Chart for Life
The Impact of Influence
R.O.C.K. Solid
The Impact of Influence Vol. 2
Kids Book- Stay On The Right P.A.T.H.
The Impact of Influence Vol. 3
Black Men Love
The Impact of Influence Vol. 4
The Winning Mindset
The Impact of Influence Vol. 5

FOSTERING POSITIVE PROFESSIONAL RELATIONSHIPS
Dr. Denetria Phlegm

"I want to thank you for always listening and being there and showing up for me. You help and inspire me so much I don't know what I'd do without you."
~M.D.

"Thank you for your leadership! You have an amazing ability to guide people through grace and purpose. I am continuously grateful to get to work with and learn from you."
~A.B.

"You inspire me because you are truly an educator for your students. You lead and work with grace, compassion, equity, and love. You do not complain, you push forward and are always professional."
~M.G.

"I wouldn't be so happy teaching without your support!"
~L.C.

Heartfelt sentiments like these don't come easily. My success as an effective instructional coach requires prioritizing the building of positive professional relationships. I truly believe that serving others is my ministry, and I know that I am only able to serve others well by soldering solid connections. I do that largely by leading by example. Educators must feel that they can trust my expertise and believe that I value their professional growth just as much as they do. I take that responsibility very seriously and know that relationships are a crucial key to my success.

I have served as an educator for over 20 years, but education was not my first career. During my late teens and twenties, I served in banking. I methodically worked my way up from a paid summer intern to a customer service manager over the course of 9 years. Much of what I learned about leadership and relationship building came from my time in banking. I lived by three principles then, and I carry those three principles with me today in absolutely everything I do.

Those principles are:
- *Professionals behave as they must, not as they feel.*
- *It is always better to under promise and over deliver than to over promise and under deliver.*
- *Be open to learning from anyone at any time.*

Early in my banking career, I remember seeing a sign on a desk that read "Professionals behave as they must, not as they feel." That quote has never left me. When I first saw it, I took it to mean the same as I do now: I have an obligation to always carry myself as a skilled professional, with all people, no matter how I personally feel at the moment. I have been exhausted, offended, shocked, angry, disrespected, annoyed, disappointed, and dismayed many times in my work. In each of these moments, I challenge myself to respond with as much grace, poise, and professionalism as I can muster.

The trending social behavior of "matching energies" is now very common regarding personal and professional social interactions. "Matching energies" is the notion that your behavior toward me dictates how I will behave toward you. In essence, if you are disrespectful, rude, or off-putting to me, I am now expected to, or allowed to be, all those things toward you. I couldn't disagree with this choice of behavior more, especially when it comes to building positive personal or professional relationships. In my view, no one gets to dictate how I show up in a situation or how I choose to represent myself. No one gets to dictate how I represent my husband, my family, my parents, my elders, my community, or my ancestors. Only I can do that. "Matching energies", to me, gives far too much power to those who do not serve, or even care about what I ultimately stand for. Instead, I will always choose to interact with all persons in a manner that honors my values and respect for the service that I see as my life's work. Operating from a place of professionalism, despite my feelings toward the individual or situation at hand, is a standard that I hold for myself. I've been told it does not go unnoticed. My intentionality in this endeavor allows for the pouring of the solid foundations in my professional relationships.

Another relationship-building mantra for me is also something I learned early in my career in banking: *it is better to under promise and over deliver than to over promise and under deliver.* If I casually, in passing, tell a student, parent, or colleague that I will get back to them in word or deed, I take that very seriously. I am always going to try my best to follow through on my word in a manner that benefits the person I am in a relationship with. In my eyes, my word to you has now become a commitment, and I strive to be a woman of my word. Of course, obstacles may arise that will interfere with my ability to honor my word. If that becomes the case, I will communicate my shortcoming swiftly to the individual who was depending on me to fulfill my commitment.

As a concrete example, during my time in banking, I would often receive requests for printed copies of past bank statements. We had an out-of-state department that fielded these requests, and the copies were sent to us at the local branch. Depending on the request, the completion time frame was roughly anywhere from two to ten business days. Before I learned my lesson, and in an eagerness to fulfill the customer's often urgent need, many times I quoted a much quicker two to three business day turnaround. This would lead to unnecessary conflict if the request took longer. Because of my overzealousness, I put myself in a situation where I then had to field disappointing customer service and all that came with that. My tendency to over promise and under deliver caused the trust that I and the bank had with the customer to be marred. I soon learned that when I started quoting the longer, seven-to-ten-day turnaround, and the customer received their documents in three days, for example, our customers were well-pleased. Our professional relationship was also cemented in a more positive way.

This lesson taught me that the long-term impact on the customer's relationship with our institution was more important than the short-term satisfaction I got from quoting a quicker turnaround time on the completion of projects. Even now in my educational role, when I advise someone that I can complete a task or project by Friday, for example, in my mind, I've already committed to having it done by Wednesday. Under promising and over delivering is my professional goal. I will do whatever I have to do on my part to fulfill the demand because I know that I've made a commitment to you that will have a lasting impact on our relationship.

Finally, *I absolutely love learning.* It is one of my most favorite things to do. In my twenty plus years in education, I have amassed two advanced degrees, thousands of hours of professional learning, dozens of awards and honors, and have maintained a solid reputation as an expert in the field of English language acquisition for students in grades K-12. I am not sharing this to boast. I am sharing that data to convey the message that even with my resume and over twenty years of on-the-job experience, I am still as hungry to learn more about my craft in 2023 as I was in 2001. Because I know that learning is often acquired in relationships with others, I am humbled and excited to learn from, and with, others of all walks of life and experiences.

My colleagues can attest to the fact that I am giddy about attending professional learning sessions, always sit in the front row and make sure that I actively participate. Even if it's a lackluster presentation, I'm still thankful for the opportunity to learn. If nothing else, I learned what not to do in my next presentation. I also know that if I am to lead others, I must serve as a forever learner – always inquisitive, always questioning and always growing.

Further, because I love learning, I physically lean in toward people when they are sharing their knowledge or perspectives with me. I listen intently, not with the need to respond but with the urge to understand. I always try to see things from different perspectives because they are, after all, different experiences of interacting with the world that I may not be privy to. I feel these habits have helped me in relationships with others because those I interact with know that I care. They can see that I want to learn from them as much as I hope they are able to learn from me.

I began this chapter with examples of what others have shared with me about why they admire our professional relationships, present and past. If the behaviors that I try to embody have inspired and served as a positive influence in the lives of others for almost three decades, I must be doing something right. As the old folks say, "If it ain't broke, don't fix it", right?

I plan on continuing the good fight of relationship building and lighting the path for others. Whether they are children in the classrooms of the schools I serve or the educators who serve them. Finally, my advice to you, my reader, is to always put forward your best self, honor your word, and never stop learning if you hope to foster long-lasting, positive professional relationships.

ABOUT THE AUTHOR:

Social Media:
Facebook @TheLanguageBriefwithDr.Phlegm
Twitter @dr_phlegm
Email drdlphlegm@gmail.com

Dr. Denetria Phlegm is from Temple, Texas and has served as a dedicated classroom teacher and instructional specialist for over twenty years. Dr. Phlegm earned her graduate degree in TESOL from Sam Houston State University in 2014 and her doctoral degree in K-12 Professional Leadership from the University of Houston in 2019. She is married to her high school sweetheart, Charles, and they are raising three magnificent children ages twenty-two, seventeen, and six in North Houston, Texas

LET THEM LOVE YOU
Derrick Pearson

"Do I have your permission to tell you the truth?"

That question was the key to authentic conversations. Do I have your permission to tell you the truth? And please agree to do the same in return.

I had a recent medical episode that I would like to share with you. I was enjoying a rare Saturday night off at home. I spent it watching college football and eating one of my favorite meals. Late that evening, I began feeling cold. That feeling led to being cold to the point where I was shivering from head to toe with even my teeth joining the party. I covered myself in a hoodie and sweatpants, hoping to warm up. Fail. I grabbed a blanket, and then another. No help. What in the world was going on?

My wife was asleep by then, and had a long busy week, so I did not want to wake her. These bone chilling tremors lasted three hours. Those tremors then invited something else awful to the party. A sick stomach. Which invited its friend, nausea. For the next few hours, I did the unhappy dance of trying to figure out what was happening and why. Things finally settled down around 8 AM Sunday and I got a few minutes sleep. When I woke up, I found my wife to explain my evening.

She asked, "Why didn't you wake me up?"

I did not have a real answer. I didn't know what was wrong. I didn't know what to say to her if I woke her up. I knew she would suggest going to the hospital and that has never been a good thing in my head (therapy might be required about this), and I really did not have a good answer for any of her questions.

What was wrong?

Later that day, the symptoms reappeared. I finally let her see them. The tremors. The chills. The pain. The weakness. She immediately called 911 and overrode my fear by demanding that I get help. That we got help. That was the part that landed. Whether I was feeling bad on my own or with her in the next room, this was not just about me. This was about her too. We were in pain. We had a medical episode. We needed to call 911 for help.

I hated having her see me this way. Weak. Incapable. Vulnerable. Out of control. In pain. I also had to step back from myself and pay attention to what this meant to her. She wanted to help. She needed to help. I have no idea where my issues with hospitals come from, but they are real. My fear of doctors and medicine has been a thing for a long time.

Why did I not want or allow help? Why did I hate asking for it? The paramedics arrived on time. They were helpful. They were amazing. They got me checked in and pushed by the collection of emergency room patients in the lobby, hall, and parking area. They deemed me a medical priority. Let me tell you, whatever was going on with me, I would not have traded places or illnesses with any of the other people waiting. They were also suffering.

Through the hours, days, and nights of blood drawing, IV changing, EKG tests, x-rays, more blood tests, medicine doses, samples, and prescriptions, my wife sat there on watch. She held court, was the note taker, greeter, adviser, judge, and grand overseer to everything and anything that happened in that room. She took the name of every nurse, EMT, doctor, intern, and medical professional that stepped one foot in that room to lay a single finger on me for any reason. She rattled off my medical history, my allergies, my diet, and my suffering. She made sure that she asked questions about the meds, how they would interact, and their hopeful impact on me and my sickness. There were no secrets in the room, and she was a pillar of strength. She only cared that I got better quickly.

She became an expert on each med they suggested, she asked about dosage and side effects. She corrected the professionals when information was wrong or unclear. She did not care about anything but healing. It was impressive and important. She knew everything. It was the only way I was going to get through this. It was the only way we were going to get through this.

This was monumental. Someone knowing everything about me. EVERYTHING. She had heard it all. Every question about habits, tendencies, and history. In trying to find out what was wrong, these professionals had to ask everything, know everything, to fix everything. It was humbling and frightening. It was also freeing. I could and should not have any secrets with them or her. It was mandatory. For me to carry on, heal up, and get better, I had to open myself up to those who mattered. I had to tell them everything or I wouldn't get better. I needed the truth.

One of the doctors asked me "If I would be honest with him?" I paused. I smiled. I said "Yes."

It was my sign. I answered each of his questions quickly and honestly. I felt free in letting him know what he needed to know to help me. I never once worried about my answers in front of my wife because I knew that she needed to know them if she didn't already know. I was helping them. I was helping us. I was helping myself.

Three weeks later, I was on the mend. I knew what my medical issues were and what I needed to do to make myself better. It was humbling to be told to change my diet, my work schedule, and my rest. I had to be aware of what I ate and what it did to me. No worries, that wife of mine is the great gatekeeper. She knows what I need to do and has no problem telling me to do so. She does it from the greatest love, and once I accepted that, it became much easier to handle.

She knows the truth. I know the truth. We know the truth. If I want to be around for a while, I need to take better care of myself.

She is there to help me do so. It's necessary for her to know everything. It should be necessary for me to share it with her.

I challenge you to use this question when engaging people, you meet and people that matter. Do I have your permission to tell you the truth? It will open the door to better conversations, greater awareness, and much simpler relationships.

Are you married? Do you want to be? Are you seeing anyone else? Do you have any kids? Are you mean? What do you want this to be?

How much does the job pay? When will I get paid? How many hours are you expecting me to work? What exactly is the job?

This conversation and relationship starter sets people up with the freedom to have authentic conversations. It sets the standard for truth being important and present. It is a fantastic GPS for setting goals and directions going forward. It also demands rerouting if truth is absent.

Imagine being free to ask the question you really want answered. We all deserve the truth. We all deserve the right and responsibility to tell our truth. I can tell you some of the horror stories my friends share with me. I can share some of my own from back in the day. I did not honor this GPS; I can promise you that. I wish that I had.

Being single was never having to say I am sorry. It also meant that I chose to never share those dark corners where truth lives. Yes, I openly shared the good stuff. The fun stuff. The endearing stuff. But I never shared the flaws or the mistakes. I was afraid.

You probably can immediately think of a moment when you were at a crossroads in your life, relationship, or job. I was a great boyfriend. I am not sure that I was ever a great partner. Partners require truth and commitment and a tether that keeps the two people connected. That tether is often tied to the truth. It requires concrete. Solid. Strong. Powerful. Immobile. In my past, I have been told that I made people feel replaceable. I was told that I did not seem like the marrying type. At all. Those things were and are not true. I had to change my actions and thinking. That changed everything.

When singles meet one another, (especially in today's social media and dating apps world) it is rare that the real person is shown or introduced. The best photos. The best lighting. The best locations. Everyone at their best. Here I am! Spectacular! The best makeup. The best outfits. The best two of twenty pictures taken. We know that we are not only the best in us, but also the worst in us. Most relationships fail or succeed based on the flaws of the two and how they are dealt with.

The truth must be the first and main thing. Your closest friends are the people who have seen you at your worst and love you anyway. They call you on your bs and hug you immediately afterwards. They know your flaws and work hard to help you get past them. They have seen you at rock bottom and are probably the reason you bounced back. If only we would apply those things to love. There are a hundred quotes and sayings about "You never really know a person until…" Lived together. Travelled together. Gone grocery shopping together. An important one is "You never really know a person until they tell you the truth."

I have had live-in girlfriends who never saw me sick. They never got to see me at my worst. I did not try to hide anything from them, it just never showed up. I saw them without makeup. I saw them wearing nothing but my softball jerseys and t-shirts. I saw them the morning after a full party night looking like a racoon with fiercely running eyeliner. It did not matter. I saw them in full. They never got that opportunity. I was too busy holding it together. I owe them an apology. They never had the chance to see me in full. Good and bad. Best and worst.

I offer you this. Let people who want to love you, love you. As you are. In full. We miss many opportunities to have authentic love in our lives because we spend so much of our time hiding our authentic selves or pieces of ourselves. We get sixty percent love because we only share sixty percent of who we are, hiding truths, denying ourselves, and running from the opportunities to let people in.

It isn't that our flaws are deal breakers. It's that we allow our flaws to break deals. Put down your fear of self and let the people trying to love you do that. I know that it may be frightening at first, but once you cross that bridge, it usually becomes easier on the other side. My mother used to say this, and I never quite got it until later in life.

"Any person who would run from love because of your flaws isn't the one to love you anyway. Find you someone who wants to know them. They will help you past them."

Go on mom, with your bad self.
    Let them love you.

ABOUT THE AUTHOR:

Social Media:
IG @derrickpearson
FB @derrick.pearson.5
Email pearsonderrick@aol.com

Derrick Pearson- Sports Radio Station Owner KNTK-FM Lincoln, Nebraska. Co-Host "Old School with Jay Foreman" "DP One on One" at 93.7 The Ticket FM Lincoln, Nebraska. Speaker-TEDxLander May 2019. The love Project Speaker-TEDxDeerPark March 2020. An American Face 9X Amazon Best Selling Author "The Impact of Influence, (Volumes 1, 2, 4, & 5), Rebuilt Through Recovery, Black Men Love, The Winning Mindset.

Derrick "DP" Pearson brings his unique brand of energy to The Ticket's programming and direction. DP has spent stops during his career as a sportscaster, radio and television host, writer, manager, and high school coach. That career has taken him nationwide, including Washington, DC, Charlotte, Los Angeles, Salt Lake City, and Atlanta. In addition to his media and coaching ventures, he also helped establish Fat Guy Charities in Charlotte, an NFL Charity, and developed LovePrints, a national mentor program that promotes Loving and Learning through Sports. DP joins Jay Foreman every weekday from 8:00 am – 10:00 am. One on One with DP airs weekdays from 10:00 – 11:00 each weekday morning.

STRENGTH OF YOUR PILLARS
Desmond Jones

Relationships are the glue that binds our lives together. Every day, we go out and live according to the relationships that we have made, and for the ones that we plan to make. What is a relationship?

According to Merriam-Webster a relationship is defined as 'the way in which two or more concepts, objects, or people are connected, or the state of being connected.'

When we think about relationships, we think about our connections and what role those connections play in our lives. We ask ourselves questions like "Do these connections help us or are they harmful to our goals? Do the people in our lives help us become a better person? Do you make more income in this relationship? Are you a better person for the connections you have? These are just a few questions you should be asking yourself when evaluating the connections that you are making. The right connections can change your life for the better. If you are not conscious of who you let in your circle, it can be disastrous to your overall goals and direction you want your life to go in. It is important to be able to identify the connections that you make in life.

The connections that play a significant role in helping me become the best version of myself while helping me make the most out of life are the relationships I share with my spouse, the support I receive from my brothers, and my business network. Breaking down the importance of these relationships helps me make the best choices in life. I owe each one of these relationships a lot of gratitude, because they shape my mindset and give me purpose. They make me work harder in life to be better and go after my goals with all that I have no matter the circumstances.

When we are looking for the right partner, we go through a checklist to see if that person is qualified. Can they provide the emotional support and stability that we need to carry out daily tasks and overcome obstacles? This is a unique bond that you develop with another person, it is not perfect, but perfection is not really the goal here. This relationship is about improvement. Constantly learning to be selfless towards someone else's feelings and emotions without giving up your core values. Compatibility is not measured by how well someone matches your checklist. It is a journey to see how much each person is willing to sacrifice to make their partner better or feel secure. I feel as if this is a relationship built around trust with another individual.

The key here is trust. Being accountable, reliable, and a security blanket when needed. It teaches you to take a step back and look at the bigger picture in life. You see a person at their most vulnerable and realize that we are all players in the same game. We're all trying to do our best and not let someone close to us down. We give our best daily and sometimes need someone to tell us that we are enough. To keep going no matter what the circumstances may be at that moment. It is important to have someone beside you during the storms of life and to enjoy the big moments.

As a married man, a father, and an entrepreneur, I have the privilege of experiencing lots of storms and triumphs. Having a strong connection and trust makes my lifestyle possible. My children are my greatest accomplishment. They require the only thing I cannot make anymore of ... Time! My wife allows me to take risks, chase opportunities, and pursue my passions, so that we can have a better life. It takes a tremendous amount of trust in our relationship on both of our ends to succeed. I would not be able to speak at events, host festivals, or have the solitude to be part of an influential piece of literature that will benefit others in a major way without it. If I felt my children would suffer, I could not confidently take steps towards my goals. I'm most grateful for the trust that we share, which makes my life possible.

Very few people were taught to put stability and livelihood on their back to carry a family. Most of us were taught to go to school and find a respectable job, earn retirement, and serve as best we can until we cannot anymore. There are a select few that feel called to go off the guided path and pursue an uncharted road to their future. We all have a purpose to fulfill in life. When you're being called to fulfill that purpose, you have to trust God and walk by faith. That is not an easy task by any means and there is not much time taken off; the job is constant!

It is so important to have that safe space to recharge, be uplifted, praised, loved, and understood. I am better for the community and the people around me, because I have a well of love, honor, and respect to replenish from when I go home. I can turn the world off in a safe space. This relationship where I am needed and depended on to be my best makes me stronger.

Personal relationships are key elements that get you to your destination in life. With the right people in your corner, you can accomplish anything. You do not have to be as vulnerable as you are with your spouse. You learn to create healthy boundaries that mutually benefit you and your inner circle. The role of these individuals is to bounce ideas back and forth when you're being creative. Be there when you need a friend to talk to. To be an example and to challenge one another. Some days, just a group to unwind with from time to time without the pressures of the world or worries. These are not just the people that do things for you but also the people that you want to help as well.

Your peer groups are the most influential group in your life outside of your parents. The people that sit at my round table are the external conscious that help guide my sword and shield. I commit just as much of myself to them and their goals as I put into my own. It is never a question of who is winning or losing. It is never a question about who has more or who has less. It is not a competition in a mutually beneficial relationship. Your support system should be a selection of like-minded individuals who share each other's ambitions for success.

In my circle, we help bring out the best of our abilities as young black men. We don't allow each other to slack. We always challenge each other to push a little bit harder. We reassure each other that the work will pay off no matter how hard it gets. Some days, when words are not enough, we defy the odds and go out and accomplish our own goals so that our brothers know it is possible to control our own outcome. Others can use everything that comes from our daily life as a tool for motivation. The strength of your circle says more about the men in the group, than the accomplishments that you achieve.

You want to build character and give other people hope when they look at you and the individuals you surround yourself with. We are all capable of doing remarkable things, yet we are all going through our own personal journey in life. The road is not always a clear, well-lit path. It takes guard rails and extra support to keep you on the path to success. The journey is long when you are working towards your goals no matter how big or small. Having to do it alone makes it even more difficult. Finding loyal, honest, ambitious, and like-minded people to live life with will make it more enjoyable. It will provide you with the necessary push you need when you need to believe in yourself while fighting to uphold your group's standards.

You do not have to be afraid to fail with a staunch support system, because you learn to turn those losses into lessons. You have a rare opportunity to make your circle stronger with every tribulation you face. These can become learning experiences for someone else. When he gets better, we get better. That is how you consistently grow and move forward in a positive direction.

Entrepreneur is a French word that translates to 'a person who organizes and operates a business or businesses, taking on greater than normal financial risks in order to do so.'

A major emphasis on **'taking on the greater than normal financial risks'** so the question that you should ask yourself is, "How can I minimize this risk?"

A few of the qualities an entrepreneur needs to be successful are:
- Being highly self-motivated
- Social skills
- Innovative
- Open-minded towards learning, people, and failure
- Has a strong peer network

These are just a few traits of an entrepreneur. Notice how the traits complement each other. Being motivated and open-minded provides you with the opportunity to grow. Improving your social skills and understanding the strength of your network provides your business with stability and life.

My networking system is the backbone of my business as an entrepreneur. Networking is about interacting and engaging with people for mutual gain. You share experiences, knowledge, and council that benefit all parties involved. If you are facing challenges in your business, your network may be able to provide you with advice. Equally, you will be able to share your knowledge and skills to help someone else. This strengthens your relationships and usually results in increasing your network. You want to become a reliable source for your contacts as an entrepreneur, not only to help others, but to ensure you see growth in your business. Creating those strong relationships results in an increase in clientele, social media flow, marketing value, and INCOME!

We all know that the best way to pass on information is word of mouth. That can make or break your business depending on how you conduct yourself as a businessperson. These relationships can directly affect your income statements, so we ask ourselves, what are the qualities I want in someone I network with? And do I exemplify those qualities myself? Just as much as we need solid connections, we want to be a solid connection for the next person. Are you a good listener? Do you have a positive attitude? Do you have a desire to help others and see them grow? Are you always trustworthy?

Being an entrepreneur has many challenges that come with the job. Creating a web of support, having people that want to see you grow, and offer council helps get you through the trying moments.

Belgian draft horses are an amazingly strong animals can pull eight thousand pounds (about the weight of an elephant). The interesting fact is that when two horses pull a load together, they do not just pull sixteen thousand pounds combined. The team can pull twenty-two thousand pounds (about the weight of a school bus). Even in the world of business we are stronger together.

The relationships I share with my spouse, the support I receive from my brothers and my business network are the emotional, physical, and mental pillars that structure my life. They play a significant role in my day-to-day success. Having these strong bonds with other people has helped me raise a family. One day they will go out and be of service while spreading positivity in the world. My goal has always been to expand my territory as an entrepreneur and help young men and women reach their max potential. I strive to make a difference in their lives as they impact the lives around them.

I have been fortunate enough to have a dedicated support system to aid me in my journey, give advice, and challenge me to be the best version of myself. If the goal is to grow relationships, then we should act as a bridge to help guide others across the rivers of tribulations that we all face in life. As they say, "a friend in need is a friend indeed". Whether you need sound advice, or emotional stability, building these relationships takes all the weight off your shoulders. You are strong, you are confident, and you are capable of pulling eight thousand pounds alone, but twenty-two thousand pounds is and always will be MORE!

ABOUT THE AUTHOR:

Social Media:
IG @next_up_athletics
FB @nextupathletics
Email giaufit23@gmail.com

Desmond Jones is a sports performance coach that inspires and motivates athletes and the community. He won a State Track Championship and went on to earn a track scholarship at Sam Houston State University. He is the founder and owner of Next Up Athletics Sports Performance Training Studios. His company helps athletes reach their goals of competing at the highest levels.

He also works with various youth organizations, hosts camps, and festivals to give back to the athletes and community. Desmond is also an Inspirational Speaker. He has spoken at schools, colleges, and universities. He has been featured in magazines articles, podcasts, and radio shows encouraging people to give their best and always believe in yourself.

NO ONE IS SELF-MADE
Emory Hunt

We as a human race love a good old-fashioned success story. It provides both hope and inspiration to many, seeing how one individual was able to overcome a variety of factors enroute to their destination. Examples of the obstacles they've overcome usually are either situational, socio-economical, or financial, just to name a few. In the end, the teller of the story usually concludes with some form of triumph declaring their success to be 'self-made'. They usually leave out important parts of their story and journey. These include significant financial help or significant help from another person who gave them a 'hand up' that opened doors for them allowing them to breakthrough and enjoy the success they've obtained.

Why are we so emphatic about being a self-made success story? The reality is that no one is truly self-made. At some point in time along the way, we have all had help or assistance that has played an integral role in where we are today; some small, some huge, but nonetheless help has helped us get to where we are standing.

A big part of having help is having relationships. Without relationships, you won't put yourself in position to receive the boost of energy needed to keep going on your journey.

I know that I wouldn't have gotten to where I am today without the relationships I've made and cultivated along the way.

In 2004 I was working as a recruiter and presenter for a national company. During that first year I was dead last out of two hundred eighty recruiters in the company rankings. This didn't sit well with me as a competitor. Once I knew we were keeping score, I wanted to be number one in 2005. Well, in 2005 I was the #1 recruiter in the company, and was flown out to the company awards that July in San Diego, CA. While out there I met a guy by the name of Troy Chaney who worked in a separate division of the company and we struck up a conversation, finding common ground about our love of college football. He gave me his card and said if I ever thought about jumping over to their side of the company, to reach out and call him. At that time, I thought nothing of it, as my plan was to leave the company after the trip and jump back into football coaching.

Funny how plans work. A month later Hurricane Katrina struck New Orleans which put me at a crossroads. I was thinking, "What should I do next?"

The offices in the area where I worked were completely wiped out. While evacuated, a former college teammate of mine and his parents took me in as an evacuee to their home for two months (again, the value of relationships, as I am forever grateful for Lawrence Johnson Jr. and his parents Lawrence Sr. and Nancy.) This allowed me to stay in a normal headspace while chaos was going on around me and my situation. While evacuated and trying to figure out my next move, I reached out to Troy Chaney to see if he remembered me and our conversation back in July.

Without hesitation he replied, "Absolutely! When can you start, and do you mind moving to New York City?"

Without those two relationships, the Johnson family and Troy Chaney, I wouldn't have been able to leave New Orleans, continue as a recruiter, and move closer to a place where I needed to be to continue on my journey.

In 2007, while still working as a recruiter, I started my company Football Gameplan to feed my need to stay involved with the game

I love. In 2009, I added the video component to grow personally as an on-air talent. I used to do over thirty game video previews per week, ranging from the NFL to Women's Tackle Football. One of my professional goals, and a big reason why I started adding video to my website, was to be a college football color analyst on a broadcast.

Fast forward to 2015, as with many people on their respective journey, I started to feel stuck in neutral in terms of growth. I was feeling as if nothing was going to happen within this on-air talent space. I received a call out of the blue from Rich Daniel, who is the General Manager of the D.C. Divas Women's Tackle Football team. He asked if I could do a video preview for their upcoming playoff game, which would be on local TV in Washington D.C.

Ever so inquisitive, I asked Rich if the broadcaster had already found its analysts for the game? He said he'd call and find out. Within twenty minutes he called back and said they didn't, but "I told them you would be perfect for the role because you have great knowledge of the Women's game and you've been doing videos for years."

He put me in contact with Synthesis Productions owner B.J. Koubaroulis, who was excited to have me on the broadcast. Now granted, this was my first ever opportunity to be an actual color analyst on a football game. This wouldn't have happened if I didn't have a prior relationship with Rich Daniel, who was fond of my work. I ended up working with seasoned play-by-play guy and Sirius XM Radio host Jeremy Huber. He helped me ease into the role and get more comfortable as the game went on. Afterwards, word got back to B.J. that the broadcast was a hit. With the assistance of Jeremy, B.J. asked if I would be interested in being the color analyst on college football games that upcoming season.

Once again, relationships I cultivated gave me the hand up necessary to move forward on my journey. B.J. and Jeremy played a major role in my growth and development as a college football color analyst, which I am still enjoying today.

Growth has always been my foundation that everything is built upon. I was growing in my field as a writer and now college football color analyst. The next step for me was growth within the football industry itself. I was becoming more on the scene at live events outside of the games I broadcasted for both college and professional games.

I used to apply for credentials to major colleges and NFL teams to come and cover the game from a traditional media perspective. I was always met with denials. Either my outlet wasn't big enough, or I wasn't established enough to obtain approval. Instead, I started applying to smaller colleges and attending off-schedule events involving the NFL like the Pro Football Hall of Fame events.

Because I was always at some small college campus on a Saturday when I wasn't broadcasting, I became a familiar face and name to many of those who worked at the university. To the fans, I became the go-to for small college football information and players, interviewing head coaches as well. At Princeton University, because I was there so much, I was able to develop a great relationship with Mike Cerullo. He was the point of contact at the time to apply for credentials and interview requests. Mike always had positive words of encouragement for me. He understood what I was doing and really appreciated the support of Princeton Football.

Let's put a pin in that for a minute.

I also used to attend the Pro Football Hall of Fame events every August, where I would be a part of the media scrum interviewing the newest class of Hall of Fame inductees. While being a part of the madness that is media day at these events, I was able to meet a guy by the name of Corry Rush. At the time, he worked in the NFL's main office on Park Avenue. He was down to earth and a former college athlete like I was. We had a lot in common, hit it off well, and exchanged contact information. I was told to keep in touch.

During this time, I was having issues obtaining press credentials to cover NFL teams and practices, because of the nature of my outlet, which wasn't a traditional outlet that had been around for over twenty years.

I reached out to the New York Giants and as I was researching the person of contact, I saw a name that I recognized: Corry Rush. I had been denied many times by the Giants because they never had heard of me or Football Gameplan. Corry did though. Because of that relationship cultivated two years prior, I was able to attend and cover an NFL team for the first time.

However, being allowed access to an NFL team wasn't the end of my issues. I was still getting denied credentials to cover major events like the NFL Draft and Scouting Combine, two major events that I dreamed of covering and being a part of.

At that time, I got an email from Mike Cerullo (remember him?) informing me that he was no longer at Princeton. He had taken a job with the NFL's Park Avenue offices. A year later, still being denied access to the NFL Draft and Combine, I reached out to Mike and vented my frustrations. He invited me to lunch at the NFL office, where I had lunch with him and Samantha Rapport, who also worked at the NFL office. What's cool about this meeting is that Samantha knew who I was because she played Women's Tackle Football and knew about my work in that arena. Here I was sitting with two people who I met during my journey that knew me, and knew of me, because of my work.

Because of those relationships and that lunch meeting on Park Avenue, a few months later I finally got approved to cover the Scouting Combine and the NFL Draft.

It is because of these three encounters that I understood the value of relationship building and relationship nurturing. You never know when the help will come or who it will come from.

People see me today on many different TV networks and outlets broadcasting games, giving analysis, and being active at every football related event and will come up to me. They'll say that they saw my start on YouTube, and to see where I am now, that I'm a self-made success story. I quickly interject and say that is far from the case. I had a lot of help along the way and what you currently see is the byproduct of help from others.

A self-made person does not exist. We all need help and should help others. It's the power of relationships that makes us whole.

ABOUT THE AUTHOR:

Social Media:
IG @FootballGameplan
Email ehunt@footballgameplan.com

Emory Hunt is the founder & owner at Football Gameplan LLC. Hunt is also seen on CBS Sports HQ as well as ESPN+ talking NFL, USFL, XFL, CFL and College Football. He's color analyst on both high school football and college football games.

Hunt holds a B.A. in Mass Communications from the University of Louisiana. He has also taught broadcast media and journalism for 4 years in the state of New Jersey at both the Connecticut School of Broadcasting and Academy of Broadcast Media. He's also a motivational speaker as well as a published author.

Published Books:

What Did Football Teach Me
Football: A Love Story
Stiff-Arming Football Myths

THE ROAD TO BECOMING A CONNECTED CATALYST
Jessica Perez

"Hey, I know someone who…" was one of my dad's favorite lines when a friend, or anyone he crossed paths with, asked for a referral for a specific need. It was in that five-word quote that my path to becoming a connected catalyst was born.

My dad truly understood the value of connections. Connections that were formed through values like trust, loyalty, honesty and yes, service too. He believed like the leadership guru Jim Rohn shared in his teachings, that his net worth was determined by the solid network he chose to seek and cultivate. This network was built by developing relationships over time that ran deep and wide. He became invested in people which in turn created a living legacy that my family and I have been blessed by. As a young girl, I saw how people respected and valued my dad's presence at events, family gatherings, workspaces, and at home. He was the consummate connector that always knew who needed to connect with whom. He used to say, "One hand washes the other." At the time, I didn't truly get it. Today, a whole new meaning has come to light.

It was his absolute pleasure to connect people that he knew would be better for it. This insatiable desire to be a catalyst for heart centered relationships is what I have nurtured and applied in every aspect of my life...in fact, in sport, in business, and in creating an inner connected community. I am on a journey less traveled but oh so rewarding. You see, as a connected catalyst I get to make a positive difference in the lives of every person I meet – in person, on Zoom, and on social networking platforms. This, my friends, is where true connectedness lives.

As a young athlete, I could see the patterns and importance of who knew who was beginning to form. For example, when it was time for softball all-star voting, we all could hear parents and coaches lobbying for their specific athlete to be selected throughout the season. It was all about who had the strongest voice in the room as to who would rise to the top of the list. My parents, who were my coaches, were more interested in developing these young athletes as opposed to becoming the most popular of the parent group. When it came time to sit down and vote, my parents became vocal. They explained that the process of who should be selected shouldn't only be about stats. It shouldn't matter which parent or coach had the loudest voice. The important thing was which young athlete could contribute the most in the areas of offense, defense, pitching, baserunning, and yes, leadership.

In their opinion, the athletes selected needed to truly embrace the value of teamwork and relationship building as they would have to play together on the same team with players they had rivaled previously. From opponent to connected teammates, this was where these young athletes would grow in their ability to appreciate the importance of relationships. My parents knew that this process needed to be redefined and celebrated at the athlete level, not at theirs. It was a powerful moment that was shared with me as an adult. I continue to apply it every day.

From sports to business, relationships matter. They matter so much that my own personal goals continue to be reached because of the deeply rooted connections that have developed over the past thirty years. When I first graduated from college, I began working part-time for the city in the same parks and recreation department I had interned. While there, I went on several interviews for full time positions but was never selected since I was the new kid on the job. Then came a relationship that changed the course of my journey. One of my co-workers who had seen the value I brought to their park team told me that there was an opening at the small private school her niece attended. It was for an athletic director and physical education teacher/coach. Although my degree was in Sports Administration with a background in sports as a former collegiate athlete and coach, I not only received an interview, but was offered the position directly after the interview was completed. The principal said that I came so highly recommended that after meeting me she knew she wanted to give me the opportunity to learn and grow with her teaching team. This was yet another example of the power of a relationship.

From a fifteen-year career in education, I circled back to parks and recreation because of another relationship built during my collegiate years. This relationship was so solid that we became the best of friends, and even more rewarding, trusted colleagues at the city for just over eleven years. This friend-colleague and I were, and still are, allies. When we both were competing for a promotion, we practiced our presentations that would be delivered to the selection committee while spending a few days shopping together for our interview outfits. The question I ask you, "Do you have relationships like these?" Ones that are built on support, encouragement, and yes, healthy competition?

Let me share another example of how a positive relationship can lead to business growth and development. I crossed paths with this person about eleven years ago. Over time, we began seeing each other in various networking spaces. First as acquaintances. Followed by opportunities to work together on events. Followed by long hours of prepping and leading several meetings which led to trusting that each of us would follow through with the tasks assigned to us. As the years passed, we began to form a friendship, a sisterhood of sorts. This led to her sharing my resume with her colleagues who were looking for an inspirational speaker for their one hundred fifty-person employee retreat. Now, here is where the story really gets going. After they decided to hire me for this one and a half hour talk at their one-day event, her boss asked if I would be open to meeting with her to determine if I could be the keynote speaker for their thirty thousand employees for their annual quality campaign. You read that right…from one hundred fifty to thirty thousand! All because of a connection that created a ripple effect of positive impact. Guess what? Relationships matter…BIG TIME!

Lastly, I'd like to share how the relationships built over time, in social media, on Zooms and in person, have truly transformed how I live a more connected life. It's through creating an inner connected community that my dad would be so proud today. He passed away thirty years ago in 1992, but his legacy of connectedness lives on in me, my sisters, and my mom. We have embraced this message of becoming a connected catalyst to enrich lives and grow together as a community instead of apart. I have always sought to be a part of a community but more recently I have chosen to build and create one that activates our souls. We are all better when we collaborate and value each other's strengths collectively.

One of my current passion projects includes a network marketing opportunity that fills lots of buckets: my wellness, my income, my community, my travel, my relationship, and yes, my positive impact one too. You see, I met this true connector at a running event. Literally as she was running in the race and I was running the logistics of that same race, our paths collided. It was the mutual love of connecting that drew us together in that moment and laid the foundation for a lifetime friendship and a business partnership to be explored. Talk about a full circle moment! My net worth is most definitely a reflection of my NETWORK. Once again, let me say, relationships matter. They are the single most valuable of all our resources and fostering them is what will make a difference in every person you meet.

I am very grateful to have connected with Charles, who I met through Chip Baker. Becoming that connected catalyst has taken me on an amazing path…one that you can also choose. It's one less traveled as it takes time to build, but oh so worth it when you do.

ABOUT THE AUTHOR:

Social Media:
IG @jessica_jlo_perez
FB @JessicaJLoPerez
Email perezjess141@gmail.com

Jessica Perez is a fourth-generation native of Tampa, FL who still lives, serves, and influences there. She grew up in a family-centered community that instilled the values of connection, relationships, loyalty, and impact. Jessica is a product of that "you can do anything" mindset, and she began a leaping journey to take on massive challenges in academics and athletics while growing through them.

Jessica graduated from St. Thomas University as a two-sport collegiate athlete and began her career in education as a physical educator, athletic director, and coach in private, public, and charter schools for eleven years. She co-founded Trinity School for Children in Tampa. She also dove into the non-profit world as a co-founder of CANDO Sports, Inc. over twenty-five years ago and still serves on their board. From education to local government, Jessica began a career with the City of Tampa as a Parks and Recreation professional. Her tenure included serving as manager for over two hundred employees, overseeing parks, a marina, community centers, pools, and art studios.

After a great career in both education and parks and recreation, Jessica dove into the world of entrepreneurism and network marketing. She has become a leader in her publicly traded wellness company named LifeVantage (LFVN) and is actively pursuing to speak, educate, and lead the charge in pioneering nutrigenomics while growing a leveraged global business. In addition, she is a certified trainer with the Positive Coaching Alliance and has delivered over four hundred workshops on the topics of leadership, coaching, and character development. She is much sought after as a coach, consultant, and catalyst for change.

MENTORING & BUILDING STRONG RELATIONSHIPS
Kenneth Wilson

As a young man I was able to experience the immense impact of relationships, both positive and negative. My father was not in my life. I knew who he was, and we would see each other sparingly. I was never able to develop a positive relationship with him. I did not get to experience him as a role model. In fact, I experienced the complete opposite from him. I learned what not to do, and I had an idea of the type of man I did not want to become. Fortunately for me I had my grandfather. He was a great family man, and a highly respected member of his community. I looked up to him and loved him so much. I wanted to look and talk just like him. Till this day I even use the same cologne and grooming products he used. He gave me the roadmap for how to be a man.

My experiences with my father and grandfather gave me a unique perspective on life. By my late teenage years, I fully experienced both sides of the coin of manhood. Though I did not realize it at the time, this gave me an incredible advantage. I grew up in a community of boys without fathers and male role models. I was able to identify how important having a positive man was in a boy's life. I could see the difference in how the boys would act when men came around the neighborhood, whether they were positive or negative influences. They were sponges and would soak up all the information and presence they could. They would try to impress the men and show off. The attention was also intoxicating for them. Sadly, most of the men that came around were negative influences. This only fueled the negativity and toxic environments the boys would see, and they began going down the wrong path. They didn't know another way. They didn't have men like my grandfather to show them different.

My senior year in high school I was introduced to a mentoring program that allowed seniors to work with elementary school children. Before this, I had never heard of mentoring or what it was about. I immediately jumped at the opportunity and volunteered to become a student mentor. The experience didn't last long since the program fizzled out at the end of the school year. By that time I was hooked! I loved my time with the kids. I was able to see the real impact with the kids. They would get so happy when the "big kids" showed up. They would be so fascinated by us. The teachers even told us how they would behave positively so we could show up.

Soon after, my youth pastor and current mentor presented a job opportunity to become a mentor with the local YMCA. He was leaving his position and wanted me to take over for him. I was so ecstatic I said yes without seeing the job description. I had never imagined that I could get paid for mentoring. By this time, I was in my early twenties. I had been volunteering as a mentor and becoming a youth leader at my church. I had gained some valuable experience working with middle and high school students, and I was ready for the big leagues.

My first several years as a professional mentor were eye opening. I quickly learned that although there is training, there is no real blueprint on how to be a mentor. I would host groups and one-on-one sessions with the young men in my program. I would also incorporate sports and various activities into the program. It was structured and organized as much as possible. I would try almost anything to recruit kids. I would work with the families and schools to build a rapport and relationship with the people that would help in the mentoring progress. I worked extremely hard to help the kids and their community. The program was seen as successful. We received more funding and expanded into other locations and mentoring models, including programs in the schools.

Although the program was successful on paper, I did not feel the same way. It felt so shallow for me. I spent too much time in meetings and writing reports. The conversations about funding and support overshadowed the needs of the children. I had to spend a lot of time planning, and not enough time with the kids. By this time, I had been professionally mentoring for a couple of years, and I thought I was experiencing burnout. I even began to look for other jobs.

One conversation with a coworker changed everything for me. I was venting some of my frustrations to her, and her response blew me away. She said, "The kids love you. They just want to be around you."

Her words swam around in my head for several months. I did not understand WHY the kids just wanted to be around me. I finally realized that it was the relationships I had built with them. For these young men I was not just a mentor or a program, I was a part of their lives. They felt safe with me. I would go above and beyond my job description to make sure they were ok. Their families treated me like family. I would attend birthday parties, graduations, court dates, and other milestones in their lives. I was never judgmental when they shared their problems. I would help them find solutions, even if they didn't want to. I was their first basketball coach, life coach, financial advisor, big brother, and father figure. Through the good and the bad, I poured everything I had into them. We had built bonds and deep relationships.

That realization rejuvenated my entire approach to mentoring. I now understood that building a strong relationship was the foundation of mentoring. Relationships had to be the focus. I could use other activities like sports as a tool to build relationships with the young men. This was a new philosophy for mentoring for me, and it was a game-changer. When I began to apply this approach, I immediately began to experience a positive response within myself. It gave me a new vigor and energy. Mentoring was natural for me. It made being with the boys easy. I was able to reduce the stress of planning the programs, because I knew those tools were secondary. The new focus became presence and engagement.

The major problem I encountered with my new approach to mentoring was that it was difficult to measure. Funders and supporters primarily dealt with tangible statistics. They wanted to know the frequency of groups, what activities we did together, and how long we were together. I understood that building a relationship isn't always measurable. Of course, I could count how many times we met, but that would never fully articulate the impact of the relationship that was being built. The rules and formulas to traditional mentoring had to change. This allowed me to write new curriculums and manuals for mentoring, with relationship building as the focus. I also assisted in advocating for mentoring at the state and national level. I also assisted in several studies of mentoring and its positive effects on children.

For all my work in the field of mentoring, my proudest moments are getting to see the young men grow up. I have been able to witness the effects of the mentoring relationships I had with young men, many of whom have become grown men. Many of our relationships never ended, even after I left my position to pursue new opportunities. We forged lifelong bonds. I now attend baby showers, weddings, and college graduations. Unfortunately, not every young person I worked with was a success story. Some are still struggling to find their way in this world, and I still try to mentor and encourage them. I have experienced death and tragedy as a mentor. The ones that have found success in life have expressed how much our mentoring relationship changed their life, and how grateful they are. I have found that building strong relationships goes far beyond mentoring. It has now become a part of how I live my life. As I moved into business and teaching careers, I continued to build healthy relationships with the people around me. I have a unique relationship with every person in my life, that I take time and effort to work on. It is the foundation of how I raise my family and developed deep bonds with my wife and children. Over the years I have adopted several tips for building healthy relationships. I have found that every relationship we encounter can utilize these tips for establishing, improving, or maintaining the relationship. I practice these five tips every day. They are different depending on the person, the type of relationship we have, and our needs in the relationship.

5 TIPS FOR BUILDING STRONG RELATIONSHIPS

Trust is Paramount:
Trust is key for both people in the relationship. Trusting each other allows for sharing, communication, accountability, and safety within the relationship. Nothing else can be achieved without trust in any relationship.

Communication Styles are Important:
Learn to become an effective communicator. Learn the person's communication style. For example, some people have a more passive style. Communicating with them should be different than communicating with someone with more of an aggressive style.

Less Judgment and More Empathy:
Begin each relationship with empathy and understanding. Learn about the person. The more you know about them, the better you learn how to deal with them. You can understand their thoughts, actions, and motivations. There will be times that you won't understand them. Keep working to learn and understand.

Active Relationship Building:
Strong healthy relationships are a two-way street. Both people have to be active participants, although how they participate can be different. This is the reason that understanding, and empathy are also critical.

Relationships Take Time:
Building relationships takes time. It will not be achieved overnight. Remember that people are always changing and growing, as are you. Be patient and consistent at building the relationship.

My childhood experiences and career in mentoring have given me a unique perspective on relationships. I believe that every person I encounter is a new opportunity to love, learn, and grow. Building healthy relationships gives that opportunity a chance to flourish. It may not happen, as some encounters and relationships are negative. The goal is to put ourselves in the best possible positions for relationships to thrive. A healthy relationship can last forever.

"It may not be today or tomorrow, but if they applied something they learned from me in their life…I did my job."

ABOUT THE AUTHOR:

Social Media:
IG @mrkennethwilson
FB @mrkennethwilson
Email kennywilson65@gmail.com

Kenneth Wilson is a native of Silver Spring, MD. He is the Founder and CEO of Men of Stature and Black Squirrel Media. He has professional experience in business, education, politics, and public safety. He is also a passionate community advocate who has worked with people globally.

As a consultant, he has worked with businesses, non-profit organizations, churches, and political outfits all over the world. He has developed programs that have helped dozens of aspiring entrepreneurs begin and pursue their business dreams.

He also has a passion to be a voice in the community, which includes hosting several podcasts and virtual shows. Kenneth can be heard weekly as Co-Host of the Community Coalition Show, Reason & Rhyme Podcast, and The Speakeasy Show.

As a public speaker, he discusses issues involving the Black community, with a focus on Black men. He also discusses and teaches seminars on business development. In the field of safety, he is a certified CPR/First Aid Instructor. He teaches courses in person and virtually.

Accomplishments
- 2016 President's Lifetime Achievement Award Winner
- Five-time Bestselling Author
- Founder and CEO of Black Squirrel Media & Men of Stature
- Creator of the B.LIT Festival & Black Squirrel Media Network
- International Safety Expert and Community Advocate

THE PSYCHOLOGY OF RELATIONSHIPS
Kristen Davis

Relationships are a huge part of daily life for most humans, even animals. Studies show that human interaction is a key factor in our mental health. Relationships are vital for mental health for most people. Therefore, human interaction is almost guaranteed. Because of that, it is important to look closely at how they can affect us in our day-to-day lives.

Relationships affect the way that we see the world as well as the way that we interact with others. Many times, we think of relationships as something that only adults experience. We tend to associate the word with romance. That is definitely a big part of the relationships that shape our daily interactions and attitudes. However, relationships start way before that. Our first relationships usually start when we are born. As a therapist, I can say that most issues are traced back to relational issues as a child. Additionally, in most fields of human study, we find that our childhood is when we are shaped the most in personality, mental health, and socialization. That suggests that many of our most important relationships are those from our childhood. Because of this, I think it is best to start by talking about our relationships with our parents and how they can have lasting effects.

From an evolutionary perspective, our parents or caretakers are everything to us as babies and small children. Our most important relationships are usually with them. Our caretakers oversee every aspect of our development. They make sure that we are fed, clothed, and are healthy. They also teach us emotional connections. The interactions with parents and caretakers are what can shape your outlook on other people as well. Even though the phrases "mommy issues" and "daddy issues" are commonly overused, it still has some validity involved. Caretakers and parents teach you how to parent and give you relationship modeling. This is because we tend to imitate what is around us. Most of us mimic the roles we saw from parental figures. One thing that is a huge discussion currently are gender roles, both traditional and not so traditional. Seeing your caretakers and how they expressed gender roles plays a part in how you express gender roles. At the least, it taught you what you did not want to have and do. For example, my parents both took on traditional gender roles in the household, which caused me to look for romantic relationships that also tend to mirror traditional gender roles. However, my sibling may decide that she did not like what she saw and go for the complete opposite type of relationship.

Another part of our relationships that are shaped by our parents is who and what they allow us around. Again, parents tend to control much of our day-to-day lives, especially when we are younger. This includes things like schools and early socialization. Our schools and our grade school friends also heavily shape our relationships and how we relate. Recently, there has been a growing trend of parents really fixating on sending their children to the "right" school. This is their attempt to set the child up for what they consider optimum relationship building and connections. It also teaches children, presumably, how to interact with others in the best possible environment. Our childhood socialization is extremely important. Most of our people skills are built during this time. The way that people are treated by the peers in grade school also has a direct correlation in their interactions with others later in life.

Think about the outcomes of people dealing with things like rejection and bullying in school from their peers. There are numerous examples of negative relationships that later cause the person to suffer in their interpersonal relationships. Negative relationships with peers at a young age are also shown to cause issues with self-confidence, ability to trust, and maladaptive attachment styles. By contrast, good relationships with peers in school age children tend to result in exceptional confidence when dealing with others, better communication abilities, and overall life satisfaction, in addition to a more secure attachment type.

Attachment types are currently a big topic of discussion in the mental health and mental health adjacent communities. Simply put, attachment styles are a part of the larger Attachment Theory. This theory, used heavily by child development and mental health experts, discusses the importance of how children bond with their primary caregiver. The initial relationship with that caregiver results in several theorized attachment styles that start as young children, but then continue to manifest in adults. The attachment types are Secure, Anxious-preoccupied, Dismissive-avoidant, Fearful avoidant. According to this theory, these styles are a direct result of the relationships we experience with our caretakers.

Of course, the secure attachment model is the attachment style that is seen as healthy. This is thought to be a direct result of a healthy parent or caretaker and child relationship. By contrast the other three styles, Anxious-preoccupied, Dismissive-avoidant, and Fearful-avoidant, are thought to be a direct result of problematic relationships between the caregiver and the child. A securely attached adult tends to be very well adjusted and have secure and healthy relationships. Anxious-preoccupied adults, as the name suggests, tend to have issues with anxiety and crave constant affirmation in their relationships. Dismissive-avoidant types usually are quite independent but suppress their emotions more than an average person. Fearful-avoidant types tend to be both in want of relationships and afraid of getting too close to others. These types are not concrete, and people can change attachment styles throughout their life. Showing traits of an attachment style does not mean that you will be stuck. Change can happen through significant self-work, and sometimes therapy.

Now that the importance of formative relationships has been discussed, it is also important to understand the ways they can affect future relationships and how we can work to have healthy connections. Human interaction is important to our development as people. We've heard tales about people choosing partners that remind them of their parents. However, it's not really a conscious decision, like we've seen in the media. Usually, it is a part of the subconscious to seek out patterns that we've experienced before. Once this is realized, it is up to you to distinguish if those patterns are healthy or not. Because many of us grew up in dysfunction we may not even believe that the patterns we have experienced are abnormal. Introspection is extremely important when evaluating relationships to ensure that you are consistently served by your interactions.

While the concept of good relationships is subjective and different for every person, we still have signals that emerge when we are not being treated well or a relationship is not serving us. The physical reactions we get when upset or angry are hardwired into our brains. It is important not to ignore them. There are a few questions you can pose to yourself when thinking about healthy relationships.

You can ask yourself:
- "Why am I here?"
- "What do I want?"
- "What will I do without this relationship?"

These questions are designed to do several things. The first question is designed to help you examine your motives. Are you involved in any relationships for the right reasons or the wrong reasons? Asking what you want is meant to help you gain clarity on what you hope to accomplish with this relationship. If there is no goal, it is important to examine why that may be and the purpose of the relationship. The last question helps to understand what the relationship means to you and how the ending of it would affect your life. Asking these questions and others like them will help to fine tune the best type of relationship for yourself.

Understanding how the past can affect the present and future is helpful while navigating relationships. While the experiences from childhood do tend to shape our relationships and outlook, there is room for growth and change. Therapy, while not for everyone, is also helpful when you find yourself at an impasse with any relationship. It is important that you allow yourself to take time for an honest look at those relationships and how they help or harm you.

ABOUT THE AUTHOR:

Social Media:
IG @kristendavislpc
FB @kristendavislpc
Email kristen.gtrc@gmail.com

Kristen Davis is a Licensed Professional Therapist with years of experience in private practice. During her time as a therapist, she has worked in the areas of substance abuse and addiction, trauma, depression, anxiety, life planning, Transition, Neurodivergent populations and Career Readiness. Additionally, Kristen works as a Regional Transition Program Specialist for the Gulf Coast Region of Texas Workforce Solutions - Vocational Rehabilitation Services, implementing programming for students with disabilities and providing feedback on effectiveness to Regional and State administration.

She has a personal tie to Trauma, PTSD, and Depression after her brother was murdered. Although it was a horrible experience, this has helped Kristen to expand her knowledge on grief and overcoming substantial mental stress and strain. This experience was so transformative, that it moved her to write a book detailing her battle with grief and how to utilize therapeutic practices in real life and speak to audiences.

Kristen has a Bachelor of Arts in Psychology and Master of Science in Mental Health/Rehabilitation from Mississippi State University.

BROTHERHOOD AND PURPOSE
Marquise Sneed

When I look over the life I've lived at this moment in time, a few things ring loud.

- Time moves extremely fast. Where does the time go? If you're not making mistakes; you're not doing anything.
- Lessons are the key to knowledge and understanding. Have a vision, a dream, and take steps towards accomplishing it.
- Everything takes time.
- Surround yourself with people who share a similar drive, have a desire to be successful, and live out a life of purpose.

Call it luck or providence, but I'm fortunate to have been surrounded by some unique and special people. People that have vision, that take exception to the status quo. Folks who are on fire for life and live in an infectious way. We're social creatures. We're made for connections and relationships. I think that's what makes life fulfilling. Encounters and relationships. We have to be mindful of who we're connected to. The company we can keep around us can either pull us down or push us to go higher. I like to think of myself as a self-starter, but there's something about being around people that emit positive energy. I believe that energy is either positive or negative, it's never neutral. We put out so much in our day-to-day interactions with people. In return, we're taking in so much energy from interactions that we have to be mindful of who we keep around us. Attitude is contagious. Developing relationships that have a positive influence on us is ideal. Those relationships push us to be the highest version of ourselves.

I've had the privilege of meeting some amazing individuals. I've developed relationships with people all over the world. There's a group of guys that I've been connected to for eighteen years now that I'm most thankful for. We call ourselves the (Se7en). I don't know who I'd be or where I'd be if I didn't have those guys in my corner. Our journey together begins at the tender age of twelve. A brotherhood founded in athletics. We are linked with a common desire to succeed, to earn what we set our minds to, to compete, and to be better than what our environments suggested we should be. Joined by the phrase "Greatness is an Understatement", GIAU is what we strive to live by.

With that common fire to be our best, there was always a healthy flame of competitiveness amongst us. I believe we all, to a degree, had a vision of what we wanted to do, and the people we wanted to be. No one was going to come in between that. Even someone within our group of friends. You either rise to the occasion or get out of the way. Keep up. At least that's how I viewed it. I wanted to be better in all facets of my teenage life naturally, but those desires were amplified because of my inner circle. I wanted to get better academically during my teens because my boys were thriving in the classroom. I wanted to get better athletically because my boys were getting bigger, faster, and stronger. I had dreams of going to college and was consistently pushed because I knew that my boys were definitely going to college. My circle pushed me then. It has continued to push me now, present day.

Fast forward to these past several years, we've traded the playing field and our cleats for the field of life's dress shoes and desk jobs. Life has its ups and downs and I don't think it would be worthwhile if we didn't have our valleys as well as our mountain tops.

I've seen one of my brothers in particular challenge himself and started anew when he felt he was in one of those valleys. That brother goes by the name of Desmond Jones. We also know him as husband, father, entrepreneur, and active leader in our community.

Desmond started his athletic training business a few years back and it has only grown year by year. Creating a business is bold, courageous, and time consuming. Combine that with trying to grow their brand, clientele, and produce financial profit. His approach to why he does what he does is centered around assisting people in their development. He's not only an athletic trainer, he's also a motivator, coach, friend, leader, and dietician. He's challenging and developing people's mental endurance, as well as their bodies. To serve people and assist them in their growth is a wonderful opportunity that I believe is a major part of life. We all need to be pushed at certain points in our lives. To devote your career to bettering people is commendable. As a teacher and a coach, the past several years, his mindset and belief in what he does has fueled and motivated me to be the best influence that I could possibly be. I encouraged my student athletes to take up his program because I believed in the quality of the work they would receive. I also knew the quality of the person they would be around.

Being in the business of coaching and leading in any capacity is a great deal of responsibility. Something Dez and I mutually understand. We realize there's a requirement to grow ourselves so those under our tutelage can grow as well. You cannot be impactful if you're not passionate about what you do. You have to progress so that you're giving your clients, or in my case students, everything you have in your tank. In his tank Dez has a lot to give. He's stepped into the realm of motivational speaking. He visits high schools and shares words of wisdom to empower and influence the next generation. He's been an organizer for programs that are community centered, that are catered to all ages. He's been a mentor to the youth of our hometown. He's consistently been purposeful and impactful for the people of our hometown, and I'm grateful for his mindset.

Collectively as a brotherhood, we've all seen each other at our high and low points. Yet one thing prevails and that's our willingness to encourage and be there for each other, in whatever way we can. My brothers have always triumphed over their struggles and come out on top. Regardless of the time and effort it takes, they've always pressed through and always succeeded in their aspirations. I've seen them secure jobs in their respective professions. They've developed multiple streams of income. They've moved across the country to take steps towards meeting their goals. They've purchased homes, grown as fathers, become husbands, and positioned themselves to be an active part of our hometown community. Desmond along with my other brothers have not forgotten our base foundation, and that is GIAU. The way that they live their lives only makes us want to be better at what we do. To remain the same after being exposed to their lives would be an insult to our brotherhood. I'm better because they are better. If I have any level of success, it is because they have been the blueprint, the motivating factor, and the friends who were there to encourage me.

During my teenage years I was told "Good things happen to good people." I TRULY BELIEVE IN THAT. I've seen it manifested in my own life.

People are always looking at what we do and how we do it. How we conduct ourselves can open and close doors of opportunity. Those doors opening and closing are due to our behavior and actions. People remember what we do, and how we do things.

By the time my senior year of college was coming to an end I had hopes of playing pro football. In the same breath, I knew that if that door did not open, I wanted to pursue teaching and coaching. A few days after the draft while still awaiting training camp invites, I received a phone call from one of my former high school coaches,

Coach Baker, asking if one of my brothers (Se7en) and I would come and talk to the football team. It was already an honor to go back and speak to the younger guys at our former high school. It was also great hearing from Coach Baker. He exuded so much passion, intentionality, and purpose in how he carried himself that he always made you feel great about yourself. He was a role model for many of my teammates as teenagers. I admired his patience during those days more than anything. His ability to be able to coach at an even keel level was different, but impactful. Being around Coach Baker made you want to be better because it was evident that he was pressing to be the best version of himself. Whatever it is that makes certain individuals influential, Baker has it. The It Factor.

It had been years since I'd been back to my alma mater and a few things had changed. The coaching staff was one of them. A few guys were there from the previous staff, but nevertheless, it was a new program. My boy and I briefly introduced ourselves to the new coaches. Then we proceeded to give a few words of encouragement and advice to the team. After a few laughs, jokes, and questions from the team, we finished up our pep talk and had a few side conversations with some guys. It was enjoyable to say the least. Afterwards, Coach Baker took me to the side and shared how thankful he was for us coming out to visit. He also proceeded to tell me that the head coach shared with him that I would have a job on his staff if I ever wanted to get into coaching! I was shocked. I don't recall what words of advice I gave the kids that day. I doubt it was Any Given Sunday esque, but I do know that I spoke with the intent to inspire and to motivate.

I walked off that practice field with my first job opportunity lined up. A year later after earning classroom certifications and interning with the football program, I took that job as a Ninth-Grade teacher and coach. I had the privilege of being around an exceptional staff led by men that had the same focus of giving back in the highest capacity. To coach alongside high caliber guys was one of the most memorable times of my life. For several years I was able to teach, mentor, and coach young men that came from the same area and background that I was from.

I share that story because Baker was the person that told me as a teen that, "Good things happen to good people."

I'm not the perfect guy but I know that the way I conducted myself as a student-athlete during my adolescence and how I went about my business day to day gave me the opportunity to be invited back to share some words of encouragement with my former high school football team. We had a solid relationship at that time. That relationship that had been established during my teens. Years later, Baker provided an opportunity which allowed me to live out my purpose. That purpose was to give back to kids and help them develop through academics and athletics! I got the chance to challenge my students academically and see them grow. I got the chance to coach family members and my peers' relatives. I saw some of the students earn scholarships, join the military, and start their professions. I formed relationships with staff members that helped me grow as an educator and coach. I got the chance to impact my community!

I also share that story to help us understand what was mentioned early on in this chapter. The relationships we develop today can help us go higher tomorrow. My relationship with Baker was instrumental in providing an opportunity of a lifetime. It has allowed me to make a difference in the many lives I came across during my time at my alma mater and the current high school I'm servicing today. I'm forever grateful for the door he opened to help start my career. The quote "It's not what we know but who we know." is often related to professional opportunity. My first gig as an educator was linked to that statement. But I like to think that the latter part of that quote can be looked at differently than what we are accustomed to. We want to know the right people and to be connected to the right people. Relationships with the right people positively influences what we can do and who we can be.

This journey of life can be tough when you do it alone, but when you have people that you can lean on for support, it makes a world of difference. Be positive, encouraging, and inspiring within the relationships you have developed. We never know the impact that we can have on people. Live your life with vision, intention, and purpose. I'm a firm believer that no matter who you are, if you're living a life where you're serving in some capacity then you're close to where you should be. I hope that whoever has read this chapter will be blessed with relationships that are inspiring. I hope that you will find the people that are your people! That emits positive energy into your life, challenging and helping you to grow. To find people like that is what it means to have found a prized possession. Keep them close.

Thank you!

ABOUT THE AUTHOR:

Social Media:
IG @mar_quise92
FB @marquise.sneed
Email msneedteach@gmail.com

Marquise has seven years of experience in public education, all as a classroom teacher, football coach, track coach, and two years as a basketball coach. He's coached multiple student athletes to All District/Regional and State honors as well as seeing them through to earning college scholarships.

Marquise has a Bachelor of Science degree in Kinesiology from Sam Houston State University. He is a bestselling author for his collaborative work in The Impact Of Influence Vol 1. He's also an avid traveler and musical artist. Marquise is passionate about being in the classroom and enjoys seeing his students develop academically.

Marquise believes the measure of a life is its service. Daily, he strives to honor and serve his family, friends, students and community through example, discipline, focus, patience and commitment.

His certifications include:
- TExES Social Studies 7-12

"I'm the product of great people stepping into my life and having an impact that has shifted my mindset over the past two decades. Because of those great people I have strived to serve as they did for me. My purpose is wrapped up in living a life that involves seeing people grow and develop. Whether that's students, young adults, peers, or family. I simply enjoy assisting and seeing people become better."

"The measure of a life is its service."

CALAIS CONNECTIONS
Michael Calais

I am honored that Charles Woods invited me to share my experiences in the area of concrete connections and relationships. My name is Michael I. Calais M Ed. I've been a big fan of the work he has done in the Impact of Influence. I'd like to share my experience about how I transitioned through my maturation phases of being a mentee and mentor, gathering and giving information that built self-empowerment in myself and others. Thank you once again for allowing me to use my lens to convey this message in collaboration with this effort.

Everyone is the sum of their parts. People have different experiences. The experience will forever be part of that person's emotional DNA. This is one's self-actualization, or how one perceives themselves and their values. I believe the acknowledgment of gratitude, a great attitude, and taking calculated risks is what I found to be my emotional genetic makeup. The positive relationships that I have had the honor to experience, both personal and professional, was first founded by my interactions with others.

Embodying these three principles gave me self-assurance, a sense of positivity, and self-empowerment to engage in relationships with people that put me on a successful path to my own self-fulfillment. I can remember as early as primary school when my first-grade teacher gave me the opportunity to present in front of the classroom. That prompted me to take chances to be the first. The experience was both terrifying and invigorating. I remember my friends staring at me as I recited the Pledge of Allegiance. While leading the class I focused on the words, "One Nation Under God". Under God was my moment to shine, and I did! I then volunteered to say the pledge. With this new empowerment, I took more chances in different avenues.

Connections start with oneself. One must be open to grows and glows. Sometimes the grows from trusted individuals or groups can cause a person to resist the growth. I usually follow the method of the QTIP which stands for Quit taking it Personal. Information from the right sources is good for your growth. Be in the moment when this happens. Know that the person, without a doubt, is here for you. Filter out the information that is not necessarily targeted for you, because we all have "grows". Internalize the advice that helps you be the best version of yourself.

This ties into the attitude of serving. The attitude of serving others as a giver on every level. Giving of your time, your creativity, mentorship, and resources in some instances will cultivate thriving relations. You will receive in exact proportion with the balancing of your life partners and children. Most connections are initiated by servant leaders. These are people that are positive, outgoing, and have a firm understanding of functioning in the areas of work and society. They are perceived from the outside as a glass-half-full type of person.

My First Mentor

I believe being kind and grateful brings positive and attractive surroundings. My experience with my first mentor taught me that by being myself and having a great attitude, positive people will be drawn to the energy that you exude. I met Rick at a Chapel Church. It was a youth revival. He was not the pastor, just a church member.

I was sixteen. I slept over at a friend's house the night before and agreed to go to church with him the next day. During this time, I was playing football at the high school, taking advanced classes, and trying to find myself. This newfound attention caused me to seek my higher power, but I was unable to really find it until I met Rick. I was amazed at how unapologetically he sang in the choir. I knew he loved the Lord, and I wanted that relationship. It was something I was searching for. He was loud and clear, "Today was the day the Lord has made."

Rick knew some of my close friends that were church members. They introduced me to Rick and his family. Rick was married with three sons and was an ex-football player. He has three sons that I consider brothers, Robert John, Ross, and Rustin. What he possessed is what I was missing, a relationship with the highest power. He also modeled the family values that I craved. Rhonda would show her love for his family through her words and actions. This was something that I wanted to experience.

First, Rick gave me a firm handshake and a smile. He engaged me in a short conversation about church and how I liked the service. I told him it was my first time seeing a guy his size in the middle of the church choir singing the lead in the gospel. Rick advised, "Be the best person you can be because there is only one you."

What he said shot a spark in me that led to a flurry of questions that he did not mind answering. He took his time getting specific so he could answer my questions completely. After fifteen minutes my friend grew tired of me rambling and said it was time to go. I began visiting the same church with friends that were in my town but traveled to that same church.

My motivation guided me to their family, and it worked. He welcomed me into his family like the fourth son. I grew into the family unit by going to church on Sundays and having deep spiritual conversations with the family. During my junior and senior years, I had been quite a stand-out and was recruited by many universities to play. Rick gave me advice on the positives and negatives of different universities. We also talked in depth about the area of study I should pursue.

Rick was very easy to talk to. Like clockwork, I would have short conversations with Rick discussing my plans. He would give me honest answers and ask probing questions that would lead to a different question which would receive another thought-provoking answer. Rick was the kind of man I was inspired to be. He often shared with me that he was a humble man that drew his strength from his faith, the glory of having kids, and a loving wife that supports him. Thank you, Rick and the Sampey family! My admiration for you is strong and I deeply appreciate your encouragement of my steadfast commitment to continue my journey of studying and playing college football at LSU.

This football family was one from which stories are made. This was a great football coach with a loving family and businessman father that loved LSU football. I enjoyed our welcoming family time. We cemented respect and concrete bonds in our early years. Mr. Kenny Arceneaux spoke like an elder that wanted only the best for you. He offered great advice. You are my Lumberjack/Tiger family. Geaux Tigers. I am forever grateful.

Why you do what you do?

My "Why" is to pour into others as someone poured into me. I want to model my gifts for others and inspire them to achieve more than they expect of themselves.

Being grateful takes a new meaning when it is paired with the unshakeable belief that the objective will be achieved. It takes confidence in the relationship built around that person or team. Everyone involved should be committed to the time and effort while believing in outcomes that are unseen. To achieve a goal that would be achieved down the road.

After my playing years, I decided to follow my passion to mentor youth and be a servant-giver like the mentors I acquired and admired. I chose to coach football, the sport that taught me and so many before me the fundamental truths of achieving life goals. Goal setting, perseverance, consistency, and teamwork. A football coach must have the right people skills to collaborate with personalities in the office and manage the behaviors of young adults on and off the field. Relationships are formed through trust and consistent behaviors.

During this time, I was married and brought what is now my motivation into the world. Being there at the birth of my children taught me to be a servant-leader as well as a listener. I knew that the Creator was always in control. For the first nine years of our marriage, we lived in the great state of Louisiana. It was a comfort for me to give back to the culture and climate I knew. However, changes were needed. My wife and I decided to move to Texas. After ten years of coaching in Louisiana, we decided to move to build our new life in Texas. I accepted a job as a defensive coordinator in a city north of Houston. The new head coach put a great staff together that had a depth of knowledge about the game. The team only won five games in the five years prior.

My positive attitude created positive interactions and brought great energy to the group of young men. One young man was particularly drawn to the conviction in my position and the anticipation of what was to come. The depth of gratitude that was shown by this young man was reflected in his commitment to the sport that he and I both had a passion for. It also showed in the willingness to see the process and believe in a positive result. Once the foundation was set, we built a rapport of respect and boundaries, which I identified. I pushed him to his uncomfortable limits. Coaching for me was an opportunity to help develop young boys into men. They would be from different walks of life, but come together for a common goal, to win. It took the motivation of a coach that set high expectations for them to reach their own personalized potential. I had many conversations. This included stopping limiting beliefs of themselves to be better. The conversations would take place after practice as reflections. After practice, we spoke of leadership and hierarchy. We would go in depth dissecting the characteristics of a leader. Like a sponge, he absorbed all he could, and more. This young man was not known to be vocal nor to take the lead. But he was persistent and consistently worked hard and got better every day.

Needless to say, it was another subpar season. The offseason was the key to a breakthrough. I mentored this young man to lead his group, to strengthen his team, and lead them through an offseason that would bring fruit from all their hard work. I spoke affirmations that later became a battle cry into and all through the season. "YOU KNOW WHO WE ARE!"

Through time and maturation, this concrete connection grew into a mentor relationship that gave the mentor the response intended and the mentee the outcomes he expected. He finished his high school career as team captain, first-team all-league, and taking his team three rounds in the playoffs. What was most humbling was the letter I received from his father thanking me for what he thought was a breakthrough in his son. Truth is, it was always there. I just recognized it and brought it to the front of his consciousness so it could be seen. This interaction reminded me of my role as a mentee with the people who I have known throughout my life.

How?

These concrete meaningful relationships have been the foundation of my growth. One of my continued relationships is with my uncle Irving Hughes. My uncle was the person to guide me into fatherhood with grace and maturity. I was able to listen and apply what he taught me through conversation. Sometimes crucial conversations. Being the mentor and mentee stretches you and can put you into a very uncomfortable area. Get comfortable with being uncomfortable.

He is a businessman with a family that welcomed my wife and I when we moved to Texas. My Aunt Veril is the cornerstone of the Hughes family. One great Thanksgiving, we all gathered together to discuss my five-year plan. I, being a confident man, had many ideas with great details. He listened attentively and then responded, "And then what."

It was an enlightening experience. I learned kindness and humility in my professional, economic, and personal life. Watching my wife interact with elders gave me a sense of family. My cousin welcomed my children, taking care of them and even wrestling. It was an experience we wouldn't forget. I have now known how to develop effective relationships within both spheres of my life thanks to my uncle. He also helped pave the way for my children, filling their cups with rich tradition and affirmations of prosperity. It is one journey that I welcome every day when my family gathers for holidays.

Know Thyself

The numerous relationships I have developed throughout my journey have helped me to become resolute in my thought process for achieving goals. First, know thyself. It can be a struggle to avoid making excuses for your actions. Take responsibility for your actions. Two, accept the rain as well as the sun, growth is needed for both. Three, understand that doors will close but you must be comfortable enough to make your own table. Your ideas are a reflection of who you are and sometimes, others won't understand your journey. That is ok. Continue to be the best version of yourself. Be different, be unique, and stand up for yourself. Four, building and sustaining a family is your greatest achievement. Five, believe people when they show you who they are and act accordingly. And lastly, stay focused on what is important to you and don't forget to give back to those that are willing to receive it.

Michael I. Calais Sr. to be continued.....

ABOUT THE AUTHOR:

Social Media:
IG @thecalais1911
FB @michael.calais.7
Email teamcalais56@gmail.com

Michael Calais Sr. is a graduate of Louisiana State University in Baton Rouge where he received his Bachelor of Science in Kinesiology. Michael received a Master's in Education at Lamar University. The author of Conceived in Chaos is a 17-year educator that is community and athletically driven. Calais is a former athlete and coach that used his platform to inspire youth to be the best version of themselves. Michael has concentrated efforts in the fields of Special Education, career, and technology, alternative education behavior programs like P.A.S.S., and Consulting in areas of Oil and Gas with the business of TEAM Calais LLC. Michael is a servant leader committing his time and efforts to the community by being a father in the Jack and Jill Woodlands chapter organization, a current member of the Cleveland Tx. Chamber of Commerce, a member of the Prince Hall Masonic Lodge, and a Member of Kappa Alpha Psi Incorporated.

A SON'S SUCCESS DRIVEN BY CONNECTIONS
Monica Earl Semple

People may speak of many relationships including family, friendship, special acquaintances, sexual, work, drugs, alcohol relationships, doctors, lawyers, and educators and many more. However, we choose what is or is not important to us.

If you have children or plan on having children, it is vital that as a parent, the educational relationship conforms to all educational requirements. The goal is to help the child reach a successful independent education to flourish in the world effectively. Many parents decide to prepare their child for public, private, or elective home education (EHE). Each will involve having a relationship with a licensed educator that will play major roles in how a child will grasp the educational curriculum to advance to the next grade level. That educator is trained to teach, tutor, and coach to develop a willingness to want to learn.

As a parent of two grown sons, I had my oldest son that was educated in private and public schools and did great in the system. My oldest son had a strong craving to learn at the early age of 18 months. He had a strong open mind and desire to learn. My oldest son went into the school system with confidence and embraced all learning. Cultured academics helped my oldest son to embrace his identity in the school system. That encouraged his development to become a productive citizen.

It was not until I had my youngest son that I was introduced to special education. I noticed that my youngest son was not developing like my oldest son. I had no idea he would be going into special education until much later. I noticed when my youngest son was six months. I noticed that there was not much physical movement. He was not able to independently roll over, pull himself up, or support himself. Simple things such as grabbing for toys or attempting to grab for things within close reach was difficult for him. I noticed that as my youngest son was going into the beginning of his first year of life, he was just beginning to do many things that my oldest son had mastered at a very early age.

It was not until my youngest son reached eighteen months that he began to crawl, pull himself up, or stand on supportive things for a short period of times before falling. He would slowly reach for me to pick him up. His speech was a type of "babbling". He had no understanding of "no". He did not do simple things like motioning his hands to wave bye. I did not begin toilet training because of how delayed he was.

As a mother of one child that was greatly advanced, I only knew what a child should be doing. When a woman becomes a mother, there is an automatic mother's intuition that includes many alerts. I was a young mother that went into labor early while working at the hospital. On the 13th day of October in 1993, I was immediately rushed downstairs to the ER.

What I learned is that a small strip of paper was swiped between my vagina three times. It turned colors the first two times. The third time it did not change colors. Later, I learned that strip was called a Litmus paper. It was swiped to check for amniotic fluid, the "sac," that protects the baby. I was immediately discharged. I remember it was raining that day as I walked to get my transportation. I was discharged with medical documentation that stated I was to remain home from work on bed rest for two days before returning to work.

Late on the 16th of October in 1993, I could not feel my youngest son moving anymore and felt as if I need to have a bowel movement. When I made my way to the bathroom, I remember hearing a loud splash in the toilet. I panicked. I picked up the house phone and called 911. I was frightened and believed that my baby had fallen in the toilet. When the police and ambulance crew arrived, they asked me "Did you flush the toilet?"

I was crying hysterically. I became weaker and fell to the floor. I could see the ambulance crew searching inside the toilet and removing what I thought was my youngest son in a plastic bag, while more EMTs came into my Florida home. Another worker was checking my vitals and heard a very weak baby pulse. They moved quickly to get me out of my home to the same hospital that said it was not my water that broke. Early the next morning, the 17th of October, they learned that my water did break on the 13th.

I was awake long enough to see a crowd of medical staff in position to possibly deliver a "dead" baby. I remember the nurses that held me down. They said I could not move since they had to immediately insert the epidural anesthesia into my spine so the medical staff could deliver my youngest son.

Although very groggy, I was slightly awake and knew I had delivered my youngest son. The medical staff had me positioned by the Neonatal Intensive Care Unit. I didn't hear a sound from my baby. A nurse had injected medication in my IV that put me to sleep until mid-day of October 17, 1993.

When I woke up, I was surrounded by a top team of many doctors, nurses, and the hospital chaplain. This was another introduction to a special needs child and special education. My youngest baby was alive and weighed 3lbs and 3oz. He was on an oscillator ventilator machine that was pumping breath into his tiny body at seven hundred and fifty breaths a minute. He was on 100% oxygen and was under a very bright light for Jaundice. He had five IVs in his tiny body: one in the center of his head, one in his navel giving him a blood transfusion, two in his arms, and the last on in his leg. I later learned that he was drowning in his own blood and was bleeding from the brain. The doctors came into my recovery room with the hospital chaplain to tell me my baby came very early (thirty weeks), and they were not expecting him to survive beyond that day. They went on to ask for my permission to pull the plug on my youngest son. If I did not, these thirteen doctors stated that he would never see, walk, or talk. If he survived.

"Absolutely not!" I screamed out. I began to throw the hospital cover off me, and yelled out, "Take me to see my baby right now!"

The nurses assisted me into a wheelchair and took me to my son. I was told because of the severity of his condition that I could not let him hear my voice. I could not hold or touch him because it would cause him to become very alert and possibly die. My youngest son was fighting to survive. But God! I did touch my baby through the incubator. I called on God to hear my prayer to give my son life as I cried hysterically in the wheelchair, praying and speaking in tongues all the way back to my room.

After months in the hospital, praying and fasting, my youngest son came home. Life quickly changed. My youngest son had the noisiest breathing ever. He struggled to breathe within twenty-four hours after I got him home. We visited the ER for many years, sometimes three to four times a week. My son was diagnosed at three months with chronic asthma, stridor-croupe, and this long thing called laryngotraeomalacia. I called it laryngotracemalacia for years, until I learned how to spell it and pronounce it correctly. What does all this mean? It means my son had damaged vocal tissues, with a loud barking cough that sounded like a whaling seal that caused airway obstruction. It required immediate medical staff emergency investigation to prevent a detrimental deadly outcome for years.

This meant I could not immediately return to work. This experience gave me a full introduction to aides for independent children, food stamps, Medicaid, and super low-income project housing. When I tried to return to my stable employment, I was often called by childcare providers to come get my son because they were afraid of his breathing. I was forced to resign and go through the doors of welfare.

In the beginning of this chapter, I wrote as a mother noticing that my son was not developing as a normal child. At the time I did not know it was called "milestones." Now that I know, I understand that my youngest son was not reaching his full capabilities at monthly milestones. The greatest sign to me was that my son was not walking after twelve months. He wasn't showing any signs of walking, yet he was trying to crawl. He did not say simple one or two syllable words. My youngest stayed on a bottle for over two years and had difficulties holding a baby sip cup at two years old. He did not play with other children often and was heavy handed when he did. As my youngest was approaching eighteen months, he did not sleep. He would sleep about twenty to thirty minutes for weeks and would wake up fully charged at odd hours of the day, especially in the morning.

I called his pediatrician Dr. Victoria Array on the third week of my youngest son not sleeping. She put in an emergency call to Baptist Hospital of Jacksonville, Florida. Dr. Array called me back immediately and told me that a children's specialty doctor would be meeting me at the hospital. I was tired and very weak when I arrived at Baptist Children Hospital. I remember I had a file with day-by-day journal notes. As the nurse reached for the file and my youngest son, I fainted. When I woke up the next day, I was moved to a single private room on a very nice sofa bed. My youngest son was behind a glass window with an IV administered and he was finally sleep.

I was greeted by new doctors, which was a psychologist, psychiatrist, and Dr. Array. I was informed that my youngest son's newest diagnosis was ADHD and PDD - Pervasive Developmental Disorder, which is a subtype of autism. Blown! My son remained in the hospital for fourteen days. We had monthly visits for over twenty years and many other doctors wanted to ensure they found the correct medication for my son. Going into 1995, I now knew more about my son's disabilities:
1. Chronic asthma. Respiratory distress.
2. Stridor-Croupe, barking seal cough that blocks airway.

3. Laryngotrachemalacia. Damaged trachea from early delivery medical machines.
4. ADHD. Extreme hyperactivity.
5. PDD-Pervasive Developmental Disorder-Autism.
6. Introduction to the IFSP-Individualized family services, early intervention, and Easter Seal
7. State of Florida children and family state services for diapers.

The first three diagnosis came with a breathing machine that had to be administered six times a day. There were multiple other medications to control the severe breathing difficulties with steroids that were administered once a day for twenty-one days. It was reduced to seven days for over sixteen years of my son's life and included an oxygen machine that was later delivered. Number four and five came with antipsychotic medication that was administered three times a day for twenty years of his life. Number six was a diaper service that was set up for me to receive a large quantity of pampers because my youngest son was not toilet trained until he was going into his fourth year. That was mastered through the establishment of the IFSP that placed my son into a great early intervention program, opening the doors into Easter Seals.

People will say that some relationships are vital to one's happiness and can add value to living a full and happy life. These relationships should add less stress, healing, healthy behaviors and give life a greater purpose that opens doors to communication, trust, respect, and support. When I think about the importance of relationships, I'm reminded of the importance of the role parents must establish with the medical team and educators when you have a child with special needs or without special needs.

Parents don't understand that they can create a healthy or unhealthy relationship with the medical staff and the educators when it comes to the child. The medical staff and educators were my backbone to strengthening my sons in the education system and becoming productive citizens. As I navigated through the special education system, I had my moments. I was that parent early on, that was being disrespectful and many of the educators and some of the medial staff shut down on me. They still did their jobs, but I was pushed to the outside and the state of Florida hired representatives to go into vital places I should have been due to my lack of understanding of the roles of the medical staff and educators. I had to build a collaboration with the medical staff and the educators for my youngest son. To develop the IFSP, the educators must know all medical needs of a special education child to establish a curriculum that meets the child's need successfully. I was heading in the wrong direction that would have destroyed my son. The medical staff was vital in my youngest son's life, and the educators are the most important members in society.

Once I began to shut up, self-educate myself, and foster healthier relationships with my son's medical and educational team I began to learn how to write my son's IEP-Individual education plan. I was able to help my son mainstream from many special education classes to regular education. He graduated in 2014 in Alexandria, VA, without a diploma labeled "Special Education". My son enrolled in a barbering trade school and graduated in 2020. He is now independently working towards being a productive citizen.

The medical staff did a job of importance to heal my son, however, my son carries what he learned because we were able to foster positive, healthy relationships with the educators. Those educators helped shape me as a parent in the unknown while changing my son Reginald Kilo 'Banks life.

Teachers must be compassionate, have a passion for learning and children, be understanding, and have patience. They should have the ability to be a role model, communicate across generations and cultures, and be willing to put in the effort. If they don't have these attributes, this can harm children.

ABOUT THE AUTHOR:

Social Media:
IG @monicaneecyearlsemple
FB @monicaneecyearlsemple
LinkedIn: @monicaneecyearlsemple
Email neecysoftandsweet@yahoo.com

Ms. Monica Earl Semple, nickname "Neecy," (short for Monica's middle name Denise) was born in Fort Campbell, Kentucky. She was raised in Clarksville, Tennessee, graduating from the legendary Burt Junior High School. She graduated from Northeast High School, Class of 1983. It was at Burt Junior High School where Monica found her passion for writing and learned to keep private dated and organized journals of her daily life.

Monica was the owner of Queenrodney Christian Cleaning Services of Jacksonville, Florida, cleaning million-dollar homes for elite clientele including several NFL football players. Monica is currently the owner of Neecy's Soft and Sweet Holistic Organic Southern Scents. Monica is the mother of two handsome sons, James "Tank" Earl, and Reginald Kilo Banks. She is the Gma of three beautiful angels: Corinthian "Corey" Earl, Naomi Earl, and James R. Earl Jr. Monica currently resides in Washington, DC and works for the Washington Headquarters (Pentagon). She loves to meet great people.

Monica famous saying, "Don't watch me, watch God!"

CONTINUE TO BECOME
Terri Walters

The most powerful realization in life is accepting who you were, who you are, and who you will continue to become. You, in all of your unique glory, are the working embodiment of a collection of influences and experiences, and my friend, you were never on this life journey alone. We all have a story, but it is what we choose to do with our story that makes all the difference.

I was raised in a traditional Mexican American middle-income family. My mother stayed home to care for my sister and I, and my father proudly served in the US Army, as an officer and a Ranger. We always called San Antonio home, but we moved from place to place every three to four years. I used to think it was just the nature of being in a military family, but I began to understand that each move held the promise of a temporary fresh start, at least for my parents. You see, our picture-perfect family wasn't so perfect. It was a daily norm to put a smile on my face and keep our family business private. The trials and tribulations of life certainly have no economic boundaries.

Our first big move was to Germany. This meant leaving our loved ones behind to live in a foreign country as a tiny family of four. It is interesting to me how much I remember about my childhood between the ages of four and eight. I was blissful both at home and at school. I had plenty of friends from all over the world and several where we didn't speak the same language, but always managed to communicate. Laughter, after all, is universal. When I close my eyes, I can see the younger version of my mother - the soft expression on her face, the approval behind her smile, and that feeling of comfort and safety. In our final year in Germany, I watched my mother evolve into a warrior. I may not have understood much at the time, but I knew what strength and sacrifice looked like, and it answered to the name, Mom.

Soon enough, we made our way back to Texas. We lived with my mom's parents in her childhood home. That's where I learned the real meaning of family and reconnected with my cultural identity. I remember standing in the kitchen with my grandmother making homemade tortillas and singing rancheras in complete harmony. We had formed a tribe of our own - my mother, my grandmother, my sister, and I. Again, I was blissfully happy and honored to be my grandmother's caregiver. As unwell as she felt, you wouldn't have known because her laughter was infectious and like me, she smiled with her eyes. She was my inspiration and later my angel.

During Middle and High School, life lessons came at me in full force, daily. I was hurting, lost, and screaming for help behind our vow of "family" silence. Through divine intervention, I was surrounded by love and support when I needed it the most. My teachers and coaches somehow knew my secret burdens, never pried or asked questions, but always seemed to know how to direct my talents and skills into healthy outlets: volleyball, track, speech, debate, choir, weekend service projects, and more. This - all of this- became my peaceful retreat. My teachers held witness to my personal accomplishments and were my greatest champions. When my father passed away months before my senior year, they were with me yet again to help me complete my college applications and the many essays for academic scholarships.

My life blessings are many, and I would be remiss to not acknowledge the bonds of friendship - the kind that you know will last a lifetime no matter where life takes us. My friends know how important they are to me, how they carried me through the most difficult times in my life, and how they continue to breathe positivity, love, and light into my soul. Together, we walk this life journey and have made monumental mistakes along the way, only to laugh about it later. We often found ourselves looking for someone "adultier" to guide us. At some point, we grew wise enough to understand that we lived lessons that were begging to be shared and that new lessons could only be discovered in service to others.

Led by my calling, I chose to devote my life to the field of education. For twenty-four glorious years, I woke up every day truly joyous and ready to give big and love deeply. Every new school year was a gift - new faces, new stories, new challenges, new hopes, new dreams. One year, I was graced with sixty-five fifth graders. Our beginning of the year assessment had been scored, and it was time to share the data with them. The night before I practiced my best motivational speech. I reviewed the metrics, established goals, and prepared to inspire. In the morning, I had the statistical data on the board and watched the faces of my students as they entered the room. I expected to see surprise or disappointment, and when I didn't, I became even more intrigued. We circled up in the middle of the room for a family meeting. It was then that I understood all too clearly.

Each student took turns explaining to me how collectively they were terrible with Math and Science, how they had never passed an exam, and how they were always grouped together because they were not smart like the other kids. What? My heart broke into a thousand tiny pieces. My students saw me wipe a tear away as I stood up with conviction and stated very clearly, "No, Sir. No, Ma'am. We are a family. We will never have to struggle alone because we are in this together. We are not terrible at Math and Science. I will prove that to each you. How badly do you want to be successful? How hard are you willing to work? What is worth your sacrifice?"

I deviated from the lesson plan that day as we tore through the data, set individual learning goals, and created learning cohorts. We pledged to support each other and signed in commitment to the plan we had devised together. That evening, I placed calls home to families, shared the gist of our plan, and asked for their commitment. A simple request is all it took. United, we were unstoppable. Where I served in many capacities that year and every year after, I can still see the miraculous - parents, grandparents, uncles, aunts, cousins, friends, and community volunteers giving big and loving deeply. We finished that school year with admirable success as all sixty-five of these children not only aced their STAAR assessments but moved into the top 20% of their class overall, in one year's time. Our story of success didn't end here. Four years later, our paths realigned.

I had just accepted a position as a high school Assistant Principal. It was my first day on the job, and I was greeted in the cafeteria by a familiar face. It was a student of mine from my very last year of teaching in a classroom. He jokingly asked if I was there to check up on them. I pointed to my new office on the second floor and shared my great news. Without skipping a beat, he offered his congratulations and praised me for following my dream that I had shared with my students so long ago. He took me by the hand and whispered that he, too, had a surprise for me. When we rounded the corner, there they were. My kids - my students - all seated together. They quickly hopped to their feet to give me hugs, as I joined them at the table. They were all too excited to share how well they were doing in school and where life was leading them. I shared my astonishment that they had stayed together, and one retorted, "Why wouldn't we? You told us that we were a family - to support each other - to stick together, so we did. We lost one along the way. He is sitting over there. Maybe you can help us bring him back." They affirmed what I could only have hoped for with each passing year that my true ministry was about building relationships while leading by example. My honor came four short years later. As our seniors approached their graduation stage, I stood at the base of the ramp eagerly waiting to receive them. I do not remember how many hugs

I gave away that day, or how many "I am so proud of you" statements, but I know that my heart was full.

This is who I am. I am the working embodiment of a collection of influences and experiences earned through building remarkable relationships that span multiple generations. As I continue to become, I find myself reflecting on what I have learned so far.

CONTINUE TO BECOME

Compassion and kindness are at the core of human connection. It demands that we refrain from passing judgment and instead open our hearts and minds to interreacting with each other in our most vulnerable state.

Own your mistakes. It happened. Learn from it. Forgive yourself. Move on. (This one is easier said than done.)

Never silence. Stand strong as an advocate for humanity. Do what you know is right.

Take on each new day with fresh eyes and a purposeful mission. Talk less. Listen more. Work hard.

Intentionally navigate life. Stand resolved to approach challenge and adversity with grace, gratitude, and generosity. Those you encounter will know your heart and your purest of intentions.

Nourish your mind, body, and spirit. Surround yourself with loving and supportive people. Practice self-care. Rest. Relax. Recharge. It is our reward to be fully present to appreciate life's simplicities.

Unique is exactly what the world needs now. Do not shy away from radiating pure joy. Be YOU - goofy, shy, weird, opinionated, wonderous, original...YOU!

Empathy is the grandest gift of all. As a servant leader in education, I carry this truth with me. Empathy told me to hold tightly to the hand of my student during a medical emergency while reassuring his mother on the phone that he would not be alone. Empathy was the reason I contacted the consulate and drove to a courthouse to help my student and his family in danger of deportation. Empathy was bowing my head in prayer at the loss of a colleague and asking what more I could have done. Empathy was embracing our students and their families - as my kids and my families because we are all one family. Empathy was taking a step forward and reaching back to assist someone else fulfill their dream, too. Empathy is often dismissed as a vice. Frankly, that is a shame, because all it takes is the smallest act of caring to change a life forever - one smile, one kind word, one honest compliment, one tiny gesture, one offered shoulder to cry on. One.

Today, you are one day wiser. Yesterday was both a gift and a lesson. Tomorrow, you will be new and improved.
Obstacles will happen and when they do, remember to ask for help. You are never a party of one.

Believe in the goodness of others. Be witness to the miraculous. You were born to be a blessing.
Embrace every human as if they are your family. You do not have to be blood-related to be family.
Culture, customs, and family traditions live inside you. This is home, and all are welcome. Take the first step to build relationships with people different than yourself. Find beauty in our differences and build community with our strengths. The biggest mistake I ever made was believing that there was "no place for my language or my culture in a professional setting." What did that even mean?
Outshine the negativity. Positivity, after all, is infectious and powerful. Stop and take inventory. Let go of the people, places, or things that drive negativity. You are the light that serves as a beacon to others.
Mentor every chance you get. There is power in your story.
Enjoy the journey.

The most powerful realization in life is accepting who you were, who you are, and who you will continue to become. We are a work in progress and intended to learn from each other. This is the key to our life journey. We are blessed with multi-generational relationships and life lessons that challenge us, grow us, refine us, and beg us to be the legacy - to continue to become. We all have a story. I challenge you to share yours.

ABOUT THE AUTHOR:

Social Media:
IG @terriwalters18
Email terrif1227@gmail.com

Terri Elizabeth Walters has served in public education for twenty-four years: fourteen years as a classroom teacher, three years as an Instructional Specialist, and seven years in administration. She has a Master of Education in Educational Leadership from Lamar University and a Bachelor of Arts in Interdisciplinary Studies from the University of the Incarnate Word. Throughout her career, Terri has earned several awards and certifications:
- Assistant Principal of the Year, 2018
- Mickelson ExxonMobil Honor Award, 2012
- Rice University's People's Choice Award, 2011
- Teacher of the Year, Cy-Fair ISD, 2006
- Walmart Teacher of the Year, 2005
- Principal Certification (EC-12)
- English as a Second Language Certification (EC -12)
- Elementary Self-Contained Certification (1-8)
- Elementary Mathematics Certification (1-8)

Terri joined Pearson as a curriculum specialist for four years where she refined her talents as an instructional coach, trainer, and professional public speaker. She now shares her many skills with Dell Technologies.

In her personal life, Terri is a goat rancher and life enthusiast. She draws inspiration from her family of men and is honored to be wife and mother.

TRUST AS THE ESSENTIAL COMPONENT OF A LASTING RELATIONSHIP
Troy Wingerter

The definition of a strong relationship is exceptionally difficult to quantify and define. One may observe what they perceive as an ideal relationship, but that perception turns out to be just as false as the connection itself. The subjective nature of an individual's relationship needs and the environment that we grow in play a huge role in what we seek and need when we are developing a relationship. It is this complexity that creates a great deal of difficulty when describing the most important facets and ingredients of what strong relationships entail. Interestingly enough, we know a strong relationship when we see one. With so many variables, how is it that sometimes we just know? There has to be one common element present in all relationships that can act as the fulcrum point between strong relationships and the ones that may appear that way and fail with time or adversity.

After twenty-six years in college football, I base most of my relationship examples and lessons on the ones that I have learned working with intercollegiate student athletes. The complexities that go into filling our roles "in loco parentis" as coaches, teachers, and mentors expose us to the aforementioned observation that, the make-up of the strongest relationships does not fit conveniently like ingredients in a Gumbo and varies greatly depending on the personalities involved. With that said, you know a good relationship when you see it. While each personality needs different elements to develop that strong relationship, there is one ingredient that must exist before any positive relationship can be developed ... and that component is trust. It is the most important attribute in our leaders and something that we are innately born with but can abandon quickly.

From the womb we are bound with our mother, sometimes our fathers, and that bond is where the trust begins. Almost as an evolved instinct, we trust our mothers before we can even comprehend what the concept is. That is the building block of a strong relationship ... the child trusts that the mother will provide. Some say that society has destroyed that trust, but in unfortunate circumstances, so have mothers and fathers. Any proper relationship begins with trust ... trust that the other person in the relationship has your best interest in all endeavors.

For those raised in homes where religion was a standard, relational trust and faith are things that we are taught to grasp before we have the capability to understand. We blindly trust in God because we aren't yet capable of comprehending what a relationship with God entails. We just trust that a benevolent God sits up there and looks out for us like a loving grandparent. That relationship grows as we realize that there are perceived caveats to that benevolence, and that terrible things happen that aren't necessarily related to whether we were good or bad. It's not until we are older that we better understand the complexities of sin and circumstance in our lives. In the face of the growing understanding that a strong relationship with God means that, more often than not, we don't comprehend the path set before us ... we have to have faith and trust that the plan set before us is part of a greater plan. This is the ultimate trust. It gives us a basis to establish the strong relationships that we develop as we grow. It is that faith that is the basis for our future relationships. We learn blind faith in God, but in humans we are still cautious. What does it take to develop a strong interpersonal relationship with another?

We have a philosophy that was cultivated by one of our coaches but has been a prevailing thought as long as I have been coaching ... before you can get a player to do anything that is prescribed for them to develop and evolve as a player, they must trust you and believe that you genuinely care about them. The strongest coach and player bonds that we witness are the result of this organic transaction. It's not something that can be manufactured. When a coach goes into a recruit's home and sells that family on him, his staff, his culture, and his program ... trust and the accompanying relationship is what he is selling. He is selling the parents and player that he will provide that young person with all the resources that he will need to develop as a student, a person, and as a player. This is the foundation on which trust and relationships are developed. Can this be falsely portrayed by those that are nefarious with their intent? Absolutely!

That is why it is imperative in this process to inquire with current student athletes regarding their relationship with the head coach and with their respective position coach. For that relationship to be its strongest, it needs to grow organically. It doesn't have to be "all in" immediately, it is something that requires nurturing (like bamboo, if you know you know). A coach will begin to get the most out of his players once the players trust that their coach genuinely cares about them and their well-being. This is where the relationship bond begins for student athletes. Growth as an athlete only occurs in pressured conditions that cause the body and the mind to grow and adapt to that pressure. It is a coach's job to push that student athlete beyond where they perceive their limit to be. The body doesn't always like that. The mind and body have internal safety measures that tell you to stop. For them to ignore their body and follow the coach's direction, the student athlete must believe whole heartedly that the coach has the task-specific knowledge in that training, and a relationship with that student athlete that is based on a trust that the coach won't allow the player to go too far. That kind of intense output requires the trust that only comes with a strong relationship. This bond and relationship are not relegated solely to the coach and athlete. In fact, this relational bond exists most prevalently in the bond between teammates.

The entire concept of teamwork is based on the strong relationship created between members of a team that have bonded through training and competition. The relationship and bond between teammates may be one of the strongest I have ever experienced. While I have never served in the military, I have heard that it is similar to those cultivated in active service. The relationship between coach and player requires significant effort and time to cultivate. This cultivation takes time, because in most cases the coach is instigating the forward progress of the relationship. Consciously or subconsciously, the relationship will always feel transactional to the student athlete. The "Quid pro Quo" nature of the player-coach relationship tends to be more contingent on the coach's actions than the student athlete's. The relationship that develops between teammates is created through an entirely different process and is reinforced by the daily interaction of the two teammates.

On a Division 1 Intercollegiate football program, players from varying geographic, cultural, and socio-economic backgrounds begin to bond through the process required to reach a common set of goals. College football, or college athletics for that matter, has a unique initial catalyst for relationship development. These student athletes from various geographic locations, socio-economic levels, and ethnicities choose their collegiate destination. That choice is indicative of the type of culture that each student athlete wants to immerse themselves in for the next four to five years. It's this choice that acts as the first step in the relationship development among teammates. Each of them chose this destination, and all the tangible and intangible aspects of the university that they felt were the best representation of themselves and their goals. The same intrinsic motivation that directed the student athlete to attend that institution is the commonality that begins the bonding and trust process. Each teammate chose to get into this particular "boat" ... not by themselves but knowing the others that were going to be in the same boat. That is the organic catalyst for a team's relationship development.

To develop our goals, we must find the best environment to develop those goals, and as college teammates we have both determined that our shared institution is the best place for us to do that. That shared process is the basis for relationship growth. The next most integral aspect of institutional choice is the choice in leadership. When we share a belief that the head coach is the right person to guide us and lead us, that is where the brotherhood begins. For most of these young men, it will be the first time they are given a choice of whom to follow and trust with their development. In high school and prior years, they are relegated to coaches and teachers that are not their choice. Choosing a school and its leader is likely the first time for many of them, and this joint yet separate decision is the first indication that we are similar in our wants and goals. The subsequent team building activities serve to develop that trust and relationship development. As mentioned, when discussing the coach and player relationship, physical stress is part of the necessary training of athletes.

Growth and improvement only occur when the body is pushed to its limits. The player must trust that the coach has the knowledge and proficiency to push the athlete to their limits, but not to the point of diminishing returns. In an individual sport, the support stops here but in team sports we have our teammates to encourage us. Additionally, we find comfort in knowing that they are experiencing the same doubts and fatigue but continuing to move forward with us. For centuries, the bond of men in combat and the relationships that linger for years were born out of these types of activities. While combat and athletic training are entirely different, it's the shared winning and learning that create the lasting bonds that make up the team relationship.

As we grow through the years and we learn to put away childish things, we begin to seek a partner to spend the rest of our life with.

I will not propose that I have the knowledge to expound on the best practices for developing a strong spousal relationship. While I have been married faithfully for more than twenty years, I have made my fair share of mistakes. The strength of a strong marital relationship once again falls into the category of trust. While a strong marital relationship can be more powerful than a coach-to-player relationship, it is that passion that makes it more fragile. The commitment to a lifelong partnership or relationship requires an inordinate amount of conscious and unconscious checks and balances. We require more investment from that relationship because it's intended to be forever and because it's in that partnership that our next most important relationship is literally born. Now this isn't an attempt to make a strong marital relationship complicated … in fact as overstated as it relates to other relationships, it's about trust.

Trust in that relationship is knowing that your partner has your best interest at the forefront of their decision making. Trust is knowing that when your partner makes a mistake there was no malice behind it. Like other relationships, once that trust is lost, the fragile nature of an apparent strong relationship becomes apparent. Too often partners give up what they want the most for what they want in the moment. A violation of that trust is very difficult to recover, but not impossible. That recovery must start from the beginning and with time can grow again sometimes stronger than it was when things went wrong. This is something that I am grateful that I have not had to experience but have watched loved ones learn to trust each other again, but only with time and patience.

Trust is the common element in every strong relationship. With trust we can make mistakes, and our friends, family, teammates, and partners know that there was no malice in our missteps. It is the most important element in leadership. Trust in a leader's knowledge and execution, but more importantly, trust in the leader's value and care for those they lead are hallmarks of great leadership. Trust is the one factor, when communication breaks down, that we can lean on to clarify another's real position. Trust, while hard to instill, creates an unbreakable bond in the hands of the loyal resulting in a lasting relationship.

ABOUT THE AUTHOR:

Social Media:
Twitter @CajunCoach
Email wingerter@louisiana.edu

Troy Wingerter has spent the better part of his life molding the lives of college students at the University of Louisiana. For twenty-six years, Troy has served as an assistant coach and an administrator for the football program and is now the Associate Athletic Director for Football. Troy's transition from coach to administrator has given him the opportunity to take a proactive role in all the football student athletes that come through the UL football program, an aspect that he appreciates the most.

In addition to his undergraduate degree Troy has a Master of Education (Curriculum and Instruction) and is a certified teacher. In 2020 Troy defended his dissertation and received his Doctorate from the University of Louisiana in Higher Education Leadership. While Troy takes pride in serving his alma mater for all these years, his proudest accomplishment is his family. Troy's beautiful wife, Cydra, is the COA of Lafayette Consolidated Government, and they have two sons, Holden (nineteen) and Aiden (seventeen).

Troy is currently the president of the National Football Operations Organization which is an organization that acts as an advocate and voice for all Directors of Football Operations within the National Collegiate Athletic Association.

FORGING A CONNECTION WITH TOMORROW'S LEADERS
Victor Pisano

"One of the greatest barriers to connection is the cultural importance we place on 'going it alone.' Somehow, we've come to equate success with not needing anyone. Many of us are willing to extend a helping hand, but we're very reluctant to reach out for help when we need it ourselves. It's as if we've divided the world into 'those who offer help' and 'those who need help.' The truth is that we are both."
~Brené Brown

The Baby Boomers had it easy when it came to leadership. Their mentees were raised on the "greed is good", go-go-go, have-it all-pace of the 1980s. But as they now pass the senior leadership torch to Gen X, a common theme in leadership has emerged. The incredibly self-sufficient and self-motivated children of the 80s are finding themselves facing challenges in finding ways to motivate and lead those who are either Millennials (born 1981 – 1996), or Generation Z (born 1997 – 2012).

It has always taken skills to push people toward better performance and to buy into the goals of the team. But today, there is a painfully obvious disconnect between one generation and the next. When you take a closer look, you see that the problem is at least in part centered around the lack of willingness for both parties to communicate differently to accommodate for this disconnect and find resolution. The result is frustration on both sides.

Phrases such as, "This generation is entitled," "This generation doesn't know what hard work is," and "I can't get through to this generation," are the most popular quotes from the older generations' perspective. They may snark about the "everyone gets a trophy" environment in which this group came of age. Shift to the younger generation and you hear things like, "I want to be trained, not told," "I ask why because I want to learn, and they are offended," and "It seems like my value is only based on my outcome and not my commitment to the process of growth." What they see as a lack of information is viewed as a lack of deference by those above them. After all, Gen X didn't question — they just did. And they did it without complaint.

However, the reality is that older generations can't compare what they once had to balance to what kids and young adults currently are having to deal with. Yes, Gen X was fiercely independent, often left alone to their own devices as their parents chased the myth of having it all. However, times — and the resulting generational pressures — have changed dramatically. How often has a Gen Xer uttered the words, "I'm so grateful there wasn't social media when I was growing up"?

This generation has carried around a constant, literally twenty-four-seven, stimulus — **their phones**. This brings many problems to young people that older generations never had to face growing up. Being on constant display, with others "curating" the perfect life on screen, this generation stresses more than any who came before them about self-worth, perception, value, progress, comparison, and expectations — to their detriment. Studies are beginning to show that some are developing narcissistic behaviors as a result of their environment and circumstances without them even realizing it. In fact, they're progressing into an accelerated limited belief system.

And to make matters worse, they're also moving toward an infinite pattern of negative self-talk.

For some in these younger generations, the demands can be overwhelming. And as they move into the working world, not having a mentor can make these demands seem unmanageable. But many would-be mentors are hesitant. People from younger generations' sense of perspective is still developing, so even trying to understand their communication, body language, or means of showing enthusiasm, is a challenge.

The fact is, however, that they are struggling — not only to find the balance in their own lives, but also in managing family, friends, school, and team cohesion. The majority of today's kids and young adults still fall into the trap of believing that their value is based on their performance or the appearance of it. Another critical element to consider when comparing generations is that a lot of today's kids come from a single parent home and may lack an authority figure in their lives.

There is one thing that hasn't changed, though. Most young people are shaped by their environment, and they don't know any different. In the same way, older generations were shaped by their environment, which now influences the way they connect — or don't — with younger generations.

A quick look back in time reveals that this ages-old pattern is something that's not going to change. **The disconnect between older and younger generations has been a thing since the dawn of time:**

> *"The beardless youth... does not foresee what is useful, squandering his money."*
> ~Horace, 1st Century BC

"The free access which many young people have to romances, novels, and plays has poisoned the mind and corrupted the morals of many a promising youth; and prevented others from improving their minds in useful knowledge. Parents take care to feed their

children with wholesome diet; and yet how unconcerned about the provision for the mind, whether they are furnished with salutary food, or with trash, chaff, or poison?"
~Reverend Enos Hitchcock (written in the 1790 book Memoirs on the Bloomsgrove Family)

"Never has youth been exposed to such dangers of both perversion and arrest as in our own land and day. Increasing urban life with its temptations, prematurities, sedentary occupations, and passive stimuli just when an active life is most needed, early emancipation and a lessening sense for both duty and discipline..."
~The Psychology of Adolescence by Granville Stanley Hall (1904)

"We defy anyone who goes about with his eyes open to deny that there is, as never before, an attitude on the part of young folk, which is best described as grossly thoughtless, rude, and utterly selfish."
~"The Conduct of Young People", Hull Daily Mail (1925)

If this is indeed the intergenerational dance, is there a way to change the tune? The fact is that we can talk (or complain) about the issue all we want. But at some point, we must accept it and come to the realization that if you want to successfully influence others, it's imperative that you first learn to adapt and create systems designed to bridge the gap. If you don't, any mission to encourage growth and success by making an impact on the younger generation will simply fail.

Who is right, and who is wrong?
Or is that even the question at all?

The fact is that those who are older need to understand that not too long from now, the population will experience a dramatic boom from these newer generations. If we want to foster progress, growth, and innovation, we must take an active role in learning how to connect the older generation to the younger ones.

That starts with taking the time to understand what a certain generation values and is motivated by. Both Millennials and Generation Z **are all about trust**. However, it's important to understand that this isn't automatically given simply by virtue of being someone older and more experienced. Instead, it must be earned.

It is vital to realize that everything starts and ends with communication. Communication is the foundation that will close the trust gap between these two generations. Whether your form of communication is verbal or written, it needs to be authentic. Growing up scrolling through the carefully curated lives on display in their various social media feeds, this generation has a finely honed BS detector — and they despise facades, sometimes even as they feverishly maintain one of their own. Our connection with others is an infinite cycle that can either grow, become stagnant, or simply cease to exist depending on the approach taken. As a leader, you can foster a much-needed sense of belonging and fairness by being an efficient communicator and an even better listener. This brings us to the importance of using belief language.

What is **"belief language?"** Simply put, it is a way to express affirmation and empathy — something today's mentees crave. Here are a few terms that are useful as you learn how to connect with the younger generations:

- I believe in you.
- I trust you.
- You are a very important part of the team.
- Your role matters.
- I appreciate your commitment.
- I want your opinion.
- I want to help you be successful.
- I'll hold you accountable.

- I believe in our team.
- Your future is important to me.

At first it may feel odd to say those kinds of statements. Less-motivated types refuse to adapt, claiming that today's young people are merely "special snowflakes" and that you are indulging or babying them by communicating in this way. But remember — younger generations who are seeking coaching thrive in that type of environment. They desire structure, accountability, and a sense of purpose, and if those things are present, they often produce their best work. But they're not looking to be "coached" in the way that a lot of us grew up with. What they really want is to be mentored. These kids grew up with Google and YouTube to show them how to do anything they wanted to try. They aren't asking "how" anymore, but rather, "why." They sincerely want to know the reasoning as much as they do the instruction. It's not meant to be disrespectful; it's genuine curiosity and part of their quest for purpose, another theme that resonates with their generation.

"Why do they say we're over the hill? I don't even know what that means — or why it's a bad thing. When I go hiking, and I get over the hill, that means I'm past the hard part and there's a snack in my future."
~Ellen DeGeneres

So — what does a positive connection between two generations look like in action?

The answer to this question is simple: it brims with empathy. Being empathetic requires being non-judgmental. It also requires playing an active role in partnering with those you lead to help them achieve their goals. This connection is all about reinforcing and modeling the character that you are trying to communicate to them.

Empathy is all about acknowledging someone's character in the moment. When you recognize situations that may test their integrity, character, attitude, or work ethic, it's imperative that you stop and point it out, so they are able to learn from it. Everything I have written about thus far are attributes that every person — regardless of skill level — has the ability to succeed at.

Remember, younger generations want you to value them for more than just for their job performance or abilities. **You must care about them as a person before you are able to be an influential mentor to them.** You achieve this by finding ways to be mutually supportive. In other words, you must resist the urge to spend the majority of your time and attention with the seasoned and high-performance people on the team. Doing this shows the other members of your team that not everyone has a chance to be successful. Get to know all the members of the team and focus on what is unique about each individual. If you are a trusted mentor, they will look at you as a parental figure. Respond by loving them like your own kids. That's a lot of pressure, but the more you know about them, the easier this will be.

One critical way to connect that will work every time is via a simple trait called gratitude. Here's a great fact for you: we cannot experience gratitude and stress at the same time. These emotions are too powerful to cognitively separate. When we experience gratitude, it consumes our mind. It's amazing to me that an emotion can be that strong.

Why is connection so important?

A true connection between two people cannot take place without first understanding what is beyond the surface, past the emotions that are being displayed on the outside. So often, a person goes through life holding the weight of many stressors on their shoulders – work, family, parenting, school, friendships, finances, etc. However, those who don't have a true connection with that individual would never know these stressors exist under the smile exhibited in public. This is the prime reason why forming genuine connections is so vital. To effectively make an impact on someone, we must have a deeper understanding of the person. We must get to know their whole story. Once we can do this, the other person can feel heard and begin to trust you – two vital ingredients in the leadership mix.

They need to know what it feels like to have somebody believe in them.

The more you know about the person you are mentoring, the better you will be able to serve them. The best type of leader is a servant leader, always putting others before themselves. Your mentees are looking to you for inspiration and help to grow and achieve.

At the end of the day, true fulfillment — like authentic connection — is rooted in gratitude. When both mentor and young adult invest their time in common goals and the process of moving towards achievement, you're creating a bond that has the potential to change a person's life forever. However, gratitude is something that this generation doesn't completely understand — yet.

But don't blame them, teach them. Make gratitude a core component of your guidance. Express it through your values, rules, and expectations. Find ways to bring attention to it every chance you have, because once it becomes a part of who you are, gratitude becomes an attitude. Here is a great example from Tim Elmore, author of "Habitudes", on how to think when you connect.

- **Don't think control - think connect**
- **Don't think rules - think equations**
- **Don't think what - think why**
- **Don't think prescriptive - think descriptive**
- **Don't think impose - think expose**
- **Don't think tell - think ask**
- **Don't think cool - think real**
- **Don't think manage - think mentor**

You must believe that your primary goal as a leader is a calling to serve. If you have that firmly established as your mindset, your impact of influence will flourish.

"Inside every old person is a young person wondering what the hell happened."
~.Anonymous

Do great things today and make a difference.
Humbled to lead,
Victor

ABOUT THE AUTHOR:

Social Media:
IG @vlpisano
FB @victor.pisano
Email vpisano@satx.rr.com

Victor Pisano has inspired executives, entrepreneurs, leaders, high school and college student-athletes across the country with his leadership platform, Charge Up. At the core of its foundation is that leadership is both a gift and a privilege, and we must pay it forward and elicit the greatness in others to make a positive impact. To inspire and empower people who are willing to invest in their goals and push past the barriers so that they can discover their passion, find their purpose, and have the courage to act with integrity as they pursue their path to fulfillment. Speaking for over twenty years, he is also certified as a speaker and trainer through the John Maxwell Academy, Jon Gordon's "Power of a Positive Leader," and the Third Rivers, "Leading with Values" program. He has also collaborated on three Amazon Best-Selling Books, "The Impact of Influence - Volume One", "The Impact of Influence – Volume Two", and "The Impact of Influence – Volume Five."

Visit him at www.chargeuptoday.com

ABOUT THE LEAD AUTHOR

Social Media:
wroteby.me/woodz

Charles has twenty plus years in public education, nine years as a classroom teacher and football coach, six years as a head boys track coach, five years as an assistant principal and this year makes his sixth year as a building principal.

Charles has a M.S. in Engineering and Technology Management and a B.S. in Industrial Technology from the University of Louisiana at Lafayette. He is a multiple time bestselling author for his collaborative work in The Winning Mindset, Black Men Love and The Impact Of Influence Volume 1, 2, 4, and 5. Charles is a servant leader that takes pride in having a Positive Mindset and being a Mentor, Coach and Speaker.

Charles is married to his beautiful wife Celena Woods and has two daughters Courtney and Chelsea Greer.

His certifications include:
- EC-12 Superintendent Certification
- EC-12 Principal Certification

- EC -12 Special Education Certification
- Non-Crisis Intervention Trainer
- Rice University Leadership Partner's Executive Education Academy

"There is no other profession that gives me the opportunity to impact lives like public education. I did not choose this path; this path chose me. I will continue to be a servant leader to those in my care and for those that choose to work with me. I am forever grateful for this opportunity to make a difference in the lives of others. I live to serve; I do not serve to live!!!"

Quotes:

"Don't be a product of your environment, make your environment a product of a positive you!!!"

Use the QR code to access Charles Woods' online store!!!

www.ingramcontent.com/pod-product-compliance
Lightning Source LLC
Chambersburg PA
CBHW060517030426
42337CB00015B/1916